CONTENTS

GEORGE MELLY Photography by MICHAEL WOODS

Paris and the Surrealists

With 104 illustrations

Thames and Hudson

GEORGE MELLY would especially like to thank:

Conroy Maddox, for his generous supply of information and loan of books.
Marcel Jean, veteran Surrealist, and longtime friend. He is the great
historian of the movement he left to serve.
Candy, who typed this essay on the word processor, and Tom, who not only
corrected it but also contributed so many valuable suggestions.
Michael Woods, for his calm fanaticism and his 'eye in a savage state'.

Dedicated to the memory of E. L. T. Mesens

MICHAEL WOODS would like to thank:

Peter Wood, for his research into Surrealist places in Paris.
Briony Griffiths and Peter Greenway, for their invaluable help and
companionship during my many visits to that city.
Lutz Becker, for his advice and visual expertise regarding the photographs.
M. Gard, Assistant Manager of Hôtel Blanche.
Graeme Neale, Assistant Manager of the National Westminster Bank,
Kensington, who took an interest in the project, and financially sustained
me until it was finished.

For Michael Aldridge

On half-title page: A shop window in the Passage des Princes.
In 1928 Man Ray made a film entitled *Étoile de mer* (*Starfish*).

Printed and bound in Hong Kong

PREFACE

*I*n that, from the moment of its conception, Surrealism was international in its scope, fiercely anti-chauvinist in tone, and vigorous in its opposition to that 'good sense' on which the French, above all, congratulate themselves, there was no idealistic reason for its birth in Paris. In fact, the majority of its initial adherents were not even Parisians: André Breton was born in Tinchebray, Paul Éluard in suburban Saint-Denis, Philippe Soupault came from Chaville, Benjamin Péret from Rezé, André Masson from Balagny, Oise, Max Ernst from Cologne. Louis Aragon is the only noticeable exception – the sole indigenous 'Paris Peasant'.

There was, of course, the deserved reputation of the city as the forcing house of the arts, the centre of avant-garde tendencies, and especially in that miraculous fourteen years before the outbreak of the First World War, when there was a great deal of activity which, under the eclectic if at times undiscriminating proselytizing of Apollinaire, may be seen in retrospect as Surrealist before the event. The war, however, shook many of those who had participated in that ferment. There was an attempt to conceal exhausted panic through a return to classical certainties, or purely decorative 'modern' solutions; a form of moral bankruptcy from which even Picasso, for a short period at any rate, cannot be totally absolved. The young men who were to become the Surrealists were, it's true, disgusted by both the reactionary return to traditional cultural values on the one hand, and mindless frivolity of the *haute bohème* on the other, but there was little they felt able to do about it. They had begun, Breton especially, to assemble their ammunition; the writings of Freud, the influence of the late Jacques Vaché, the learned iconoclasm of Alfred Jarry, and the example of certain detached

'How oddly this light suffuses the covered arcades which abound in Paris in the vicinity of the main boulevards.'
(LOUIS ARAGON 'PARIS PEASANT')
Passage Trinité

figures of an older generation still living; but they lacked a means to fire it and were not even sure of the most effective target at which it should be aimed. Dada arrived to provide not only a temporary solution but, even more usefully, to clear the ground ahead. Dada, born in Zurich during the war, preached the negation of everything, even itself. It had spread to many cities, assuming a different form according to the circumstances in which it found itself. In Berlin, for example, it had become political, a satirical weapon for goading both the defeated military with their choleric dreams of revenge, and the greedy profiteers, blowing their cigar smoke into the faces of starving, disabled 'heroes' selling matches. In Paris, it began by provoking genuine outrage with its savage pranks and nihilistic high spirits – Tristan Tzara, one of its founders, was greeted with unforced enthusiasm by Breton – but the outrageous elements of Dada became, in a remarkably short space of time, chic. This had always been the French reaction to anything that threatened their stability. It was to become a constant thorn in the side of Surrealism itself, a danger of which Breton was only too aware, but which even he was occasionally unable to prevent.

I shall not be dealing here with the break with Dada nor, except where relevant, with the history of the Surrealist movement. Neither is it my intention to add anything significant to an already long and growing shelf of historical, political and philosophical analysis. My only aim is to offer a parallel text (rather than a descriptive one) to accompany Michael Woods' poetic and beautiful images. Tall and thin, with a deceptively reticent air, Michael has the head of a carved medieval saint framing the eyes of a slow loris. His principal interest is photography. He lives nearby and first got in touch with me through a friend who believed we might have a great deal in common. In this she was correct. Our friendship formed instantly and has proved to be permanent.

When we first met I had recently moved into London W10, an area of peeling stucco at the north end of the Portobello Road which, on Fridays and Saturdays, becomes the equivalent of the flea market in Paris. It is a district favoured by diverse ethnic groups: indigenous Londoners, Irish, Portuguese and Spaniards, some Arabs, and many West Indians whose annual Carnival is as surprising in its exuberance and inventive fantasy as

'A hand linked to the throbbing heart.'
(MAN RAY)
The Narcisse nightclub

Rue Blanche

those desert flowers that spring up after a rare downfall, instantly blossom and die. Yet even during the rest of the year W10 displays, perhaps as a result of the market, an attractive spirit of mildly dodgy bonhomie, and given the Caribbean presence, a predictably lively street life. A visit to the dry-cleaners becomes something of an adventure.

Michael, on his first visit, had shown me his photographs recording the district, not only its people but the buildings and shops, some boarded up, others revealing a haphazard accumulation of junk. I recognized, although at that time he knew very little of the movement, a Surrealist eye, and when he left I lent him two of the great works of Surrealist literature, *Nadja* by André Breton and Louis Aragon's *Paris Peasant*.

On my return from that trip to Paris that I shall describe in Chapter One, I told Michael of my visits to the 'elective places' revered by the Surrealists and suggested, as he was shortly to visit the city himself, that it might interest him to record them. We then discussed the possibility of a small book along these

Boulevard Saint-Germain

lines, which would demonstrate how Paris was the ideal city for that changing cast list of poets, writers and painters who gathered around Breton and the ever-faithful Péret. They relied on 'perpetual correspondences', examples of 'subjective chance' and the fixed points provided by the 'elective places' to help them sustain, in the face of every setback and disappointment, their faith in the Surrealist spirit, their pursuit of the Surrealist life.

Not only did Michael begin immediately to realize this project, but broadened its scope to include those aspects of contemporary Paris that he believed to contain evidence of the Surrealist spirit after the event. In consequence, what could have been mere archaeology has become evidence that, although historic Surrealism is entombed in libraries and museums, its marvellous phantom still haunts the city of its birth. In this book, in consequence, the monuments are on record, but as points of departure rather than as remaining evidence of a heroic and distant past. Surrealism is dead. Long live Surrealism.

André Gide

Portrait d'Alfred Jarry (1873-1907) par Cazals.

Marcel Schwob,

André Breton par Picasso (DR)

Fernando Pessoa

1

'The eye exists in a savage state'

'My point of departure will be Hôtel des Grands Hommes, Place du Panthéon', wrote André Breton in his marvellous anti-novel *Nadja* in 1928. It will be my 'point of departure' also, because it was there, in 1986, that the idea of this book came to me.

I was spending a weekend in Paris with my friend Alex and, to give shape to our excursion, proposed a pilgrimage to various 'chosen places' revered by the Surrealists, in particular the Parc des Buttes-Chaumont, that astonishing pleasure ground, hallowed by nineteenth-century suicides, which occupies a long section of Louis Aragon's *Paris Peasant* (1926), and which, on my infrequent visits to the French capital, I had never had the opportunity or, to be more honest, taken the trouble to visit. The park itself and these two books, together with Breton's other Parisian masterpiece, *Mad Love* (1937), will occupy a considerable space later in this essay, but for the moment we return to the hotel.

Indeed, I had signed the register at the Hôtel des Grands Hommes because, looking through a guide to accommodation abroad, I had read, 'The "great men" in question were André Breton and other Surrealists who stayed there.' The 'other Surrealists' is surely an embellishment, or so I suspect. Breton lived in this hotel 'around 1918', that is to say six years before the movement came into being, and although he had begun to meet up with some of those who were later to become his colleagues, it is doubtful that they would have moved in under the same roof. (Incidentally, ever since I discovered it in my adolescence, I have always found the Parisian concept of living in a hotel immensely glamorous. In England only rich old ladies, within my limited experience, ever conceived of such a course. Boarding or guest houses, often admittedly describing themselves

'Legend begins where man has lived, where he lives.'
(LOUIS ARAGON 'PARIS PEASANT')
The lid of a box on a bookstall, Quai de Montebello

as 'Private Hotels', were not the same thing at all, at any rate in my eyes.) At all events, Breton had 'lived there'; a good enough reason on a trip dedicated to hunting, in however light-hearted a way, the Surrealist snark, to follow his example.

And then, re-reading *Nadja* as preliminary homework, there was not only confirmation that the guide was correct, but a photograph of the facade itself with the railings of the Panthéon in the foreground, then a statue and finally, directly in front of the facade itself, a solitary horse and cart, on which is perched an elderly delivery man.

The 'Great Men' who gave the hotel its name were not, of course, André Breton, still less the 'other Surrealists', but those commemorated in the Panthéon opposite. The hotel was so named long before that young man with the noble, leonine head had booked in although, who knows, its name and his belief in his own destiny may well have influenced his choice.

I had hoped, unrealistically, that nothing would have changed since 1918. Of course, it had. The facade was much the same, but the lobby had been modernized, there was a smart new lift, and the bedrooms had showers and bidets *en suite*, and were decorated in be-sprigged Laura Ashley wallpaper with matching curtains and shiny reproduction brass beds. There was not even a photograph of Breton in any of the public rooms, nor any reference in the brochure to his having stayed there. (How, I wonder, did the guide glean its information?)

The windows of the bed- and bathrooms, however, over-looked an empty courtyard and, across it, the back of a tall, shuttered apartment building, suggestively stained and discol-oured which, providing André's room had faced that way, must have looked much the same, or at any rate if one ignored the army of television aerials sprouting from its roof. Most of the shutters were closed, but there was one, on the fourth floor, thrown wide, although by daylight the interior was invisible.

Returning that night after dinner and comparatively early, we turned off the light but left the curtains open. The courtyard and the building beyond it were quite dark but then, at about 11.30 pm, a light went on in the unshuttered apartment behind a small, ornamental iron balcony where a young man, extremely handsome, and wearing a short white dressing gown in the style of a Japanese 'happy coat', flung open the French windows as far as they could go and disappeared into another room. His

'The world is seen from the window: roofs of gray oilcloth, chimneys like sensuous onlookers; studios dulled by dusty blinds.'
(LOUIS ARAGON 'LITTÉRATURE' 1923)
View from the window of a hotel, Rue Blanche

The New Moon nightclub

manner of opening those windows had something deliberately dramatic about it. It reminded me of the three heavy and evenly spaced thumps which signal, in the old-fashioned French theatre, that the curtain is about to rise. The 'set' was a comparatively small room, or at any rate shallow, lined with books; there was the corner of what appeared to be a large and solid table covered with more books and various papers to the left, and behind it an upright bentwood chair of shiny brown. In the centre, at an angle to the window, was an easel and on it a primed canvas completely blank. On the right, an armchair of an indeterminate dark green.

After about five minutes the young man re-enters. He picks up a white manuscript and begins to read it whilst pacing slowly back and forth between the furniture. At one point a young woman, dressed for bed, crosses the room. They do not speak and might be mutually invisible judging by their lack of acknowledgment of each other's presence. We are never to see her again.

The young man puts down the manuscript and comes on to the balcony. He stares into the courtyard at first straight ahead and then, abruptly, first to the left and then to the right with the jerky purposeful movements of a bird. Re-entering the room he resumes his reading, but after a while he replaces the manuscript on the table and vanishes, although failing to turn off the lights. Four minutes later he reappears and continues his pacing and reading. He is holding the manuscript in his left hand only and then, quite slowly, as though of its own volition, his right hand enters the front of his dressing gown and he begins to caress himself. His expression registers no change. He continues to read. Abruptly he stops, and again steps out on to the balcony. He repeats *exactly* his former scrutiny. He goes back into the room, picks up the manuscript and, intermittently, continues to stimulate himself. There are variants. Sometimes he sits for a shorter or longer time, either behind the table or in the armchair. His visits to the balcony occur at irregular but somehow deliberate intervals. His disappearances may last anything from one minute to ten. His intermittent 'self-abuse', however, seems in no way to excite him.

Sometimes he returns naked, discarding his 'happy coat' elsewhere. After his next exit he may, or may not have put it on again. Nude, he demonstrates his penis sometimes semi-erect, sometimes comparatively inert, but never completely stiff. We imagine, wrongly as it transpires, that he will eventually climax. At no time, whether walking or sitting, does he stop reading. Only on his watchful visits to the balcony does he relinquish his manuscript. At last, about twenty-five to one, he finally puts it down and, on leaving the room, plunges it into darkness.

The next night, at exactly the same time, he repeats the performance complete in every detail, reinforcing the illusion that he is an actor taking part in the run of a play. Why did we watch, not once but twice, this strange activity? Well it was not, to be frank, unstimulating, more so than much deliberately 'action-packed' pornography available nowadays on video in many respectable British hotels, but this was not the only or indeed principal reason. Somehow it confirmed the day's pursuit of the Surrealist spirit, not simply as a dutiful pilgrimage to the 'sights' described in books, however beautiful, but as a living entity where desire is paramount and dream and reality indistinguishable. Oh yes, what he did and perhaps continues to do may be interpreted as an act of simple exhibitionism – strange, incidentally, that no guest in the far-from-empty Hôtel des Grands Hommes had complained to the receptionists or the manager. It would have been perfectly simple to locate the apartment and inform the police – but somehow, despite the visits to the balcony, the effect was not of public provocation. Its

Tour Saint-Jacques

compulsion appeared to be more of private ritual and, for me, all the more moving in that I watched it from the window in a hotel from which, sixty years before, André Breton had set out on his heroic quest.

On our last day, after visiting the beautiful Musée Picasso in its seventeenth-century mansion, we were sitting drinking coffee facing the Beaubourg and wondering if we could quite face up to its exhibition of late Picasso, given that it was to visit the Tate Gallery in London. Suddenly Alex spotted in the street the British art critic and writer David Sylvester who, it later transpired, was in part responsible for the show of Picasso's late works; a perfectly reasonable explanation for his materialization at that time and place except that in London, where we live only a mile apart, I have never bumped into him by chance. We attracted his attention and asked him to join us. This he declined, but he suggested we might care to accompany him to his hotel as he had forgotten his Pro-Plus, and then return to visit the exhibition in his company. We accepted immediately.

It was typical of David that he found it necessary, on a warm day, to cover a considerable distance to collect *his* Pro-Plus when that admirable caffein stimulant was available in many pharmacies we passed en route. This insistence on a course dictated by inner necessity, a form of fastidious behaviour which I find completely understandable, is only one of the many characteristics that contribute to a whole personality as complicated as it is endearing. While never a member, David's knowledge of and sympathy for the Surrealist movement is profound; he was, for instance, responsible for the magnificent exhibition at the Hayward Gallery in 1978. It was natural, therefore, that he understood immediately why we should have been visiting some of those areas and monuments of Paris 'elected' by Breton, Aragon and the others and that, without pausing, he should have glanced across the road we were navigating en route to his Pro-Plus, and indicated the Tour Saint-Jacques looming up through the clear air of early summer (this medieval structure connected with the alchemist Nicolas Flamel and largely concealed in scaffolding during the 'thirties was, in Breton's view, 'the world's greatest monument to the hidden').

We told him also of 'the great masturbator manqué' and he was not only intrigued but offered various explanations for this bizarre yet touching spectacle. He proposed that when (not if) the curtain went up on 'le théâtre de fenêtre' that evening, Alex should stand naked at the bathroom window, possibly stimulating or appearing to stimulate herself, and that I should report back to him, in London, as to the young man's reaction.

We returned to look at the Picasso exhibition at the Beaubourg. (That morning we had stood in front of *Les Demoiselles d'Avignon*, that large and clumsy masterpiece of 1907 in front of which a critic had once declared, 'What a loss to French Art.' Here were its great-grandchildren.) The monstrous but, alas, extremely perceptive collector, the late Douglas Cooper, had dismissed these final pictures as 'incoherent scribbles painted by a terrified old man in death's antechamber', but he had quarrelled with Picasso and saw them through eyes maliciously distorted with venom. In fact, they seemed to me both tragic and triumphant. Great cries of pain and rage at having to accept at last his inevitable physical impotence, alleviated by savage humour aimed at his own voyeurism of those still capable of fucking. The smears, dribbles, slashes of black and discords of colour have the urgency of a man who knows the hour of his execution is at hand, and who sings, however hoarsely, on the steps to the scaffold. In the words of Breton, 'From each of your pictures you let down a rope ladder or even a ladder made with your bed-sheets.'

So that night we tried the David experiment. After twenty minutes or so of the ritual in the opposite window Alex, naked, switched on the bathroom light and stood, but without any attempt at eye contact or salacious compliance, at our window. The effect was curious. Close attention but no surprise. It was as if he knew that eventually his ritual would succeed in materializing such a phantom. However, when she left her post and turned off the bathroom light, he instantly abandoned his solitary tryst.

In bed my friend experienced some understandable regret and indeed anxiety. 'He could easily work out where our room is.' 'He might knock.' He didn't, of course. There was nothing in his behaviour to indicate that it was a prelude to a simple 'adventure'. It was a ceremony.

The next afternoon we left Paris.

'These eyes, expressive beyond all nuance of ecstasy, rage, fear, these
are the eyes of Isis . . . of certain contemporary wax effigies.'

(ANDRÉ BRETON 'MAD LOVE')

Waxworks in the Musée Grévin, Passage Jouffroy

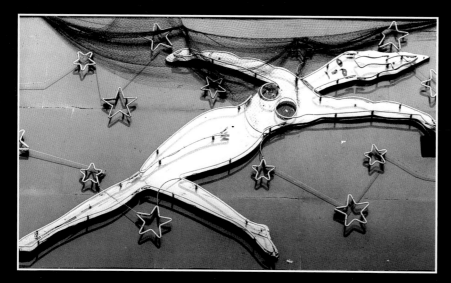

2

'The blind swimmer'

*I*n 1949 I had come to London to work for E.L.T. Mesens, the Belgian poet, collagist, early friend and defender of Magritte and, relevant in this case, managing director of the London Gallery, whose aim was to promote and sell Surrealist art to a public either indifferent to it or, if more sophisticated, given to relegating it to the past as an 'amusing' pre-war notion that had lost all relevance.

While still a teenager in the Navy I had written to Mesens, the acknowledged leader of Surrealism in Britain. The result was an invitation to attend a Surrealist meeting, and, on my frequent visits to London on weekend leave, I became an enthusiastic member of the group. This led, after my demob, to a practical development. Mesens, who was about to reopen the London Gallery, offered me a post as trainee-assistant.

I was paid very little, although my inefficiency as an employee and increasing involvement in the emerging jazz world would have hardly justified more, but I was at least in daily contact, not only with the masterpieces of Surrealism, but with a man who was a comparatively early member of the group and was willing to be prompted, when not berating me for my inability to concentrate on the job in hand, to launch into many fascinating and personal stories of the heroic days, enlivened by his heavy Belgian accent and idiosyncratic but vivid English. He told me how, on his very first visit to Paris, he had met Man Ray by chance in a café, and how Man had taken him to supper in Brancusi's studio with its plaster sculpture wrapped in damp linen and a delicious Romanian stew simmering on the stove. (That studio is now open to the public, reconstructed at the back of the Beaubourg Museum – a stewless icon.) He told me of his long friendship with the great Erik Satie, encountered on

*'Your dances are the fearful abyss
of my dreams
And I fall and my fall perpetuates
my life,
The space under your feet is
increasingly vast,
Wonders, you dance on the springs
of the sky.'*
(PAUL ÉLUARD 'THE GERTRUDE
HOFFMAN GIRLS')

Place Pigalle
The Opéra
Tiles in a *poissonnerie*

that same rewarding visit, for in those days Mesens had aspirations to be a composer, and he showed me a collection of postcards he had subsequently received in Satie's neat, minuscule hand. Above all he told me of how, in the middle 'twenties, Philippe Soupault, whose poem *Garage* Mesens had set to music, persuaded him to go along to a Surrealist meeting, an idea which had alarmed E.L.T., for at that time the Belgian group around Magritte remained closer to Dada and had mocked Breton's aspirations in its publications; and of how, on entering the room, Mesens had burst into tears, Aragon had thrown his arms round him and led him forward to meet the others. Breton had accepted this emotional conversion, and Mesens had returned to Brussels to persuade his friends to come in out of the cold.

From then on Mesens, in those days very hard up and furthermore addicted to gambling, would visit Paris whenever he could, and would stay there, 'living on two rotten herrings to prolong my trip by even a day'.

As Paris formed the backdrop to all these tales, and Paris itself was frequently the subject of a lyrical outburst, I became determined to visit it. In consequence, when my holiday in August came up I 'borrowed' forty pounds from my mother, bought a return ticket at Victoria Station (six pounds, as I recall) and set forth hysterical with anticipation. I carried only one letter of introduction from E.L.T. and that to Pierre Mabille, author of the remarkable *Miroir du Merveilleux* and a practising doctor and psychologist. His professional obligations must have explained his presence in the capital for, as Mesens pointed out, in August all the other Surrealists, like the majority of their fellow Parisians, would be out of town. I wasn't especially worried. For one thing, Breton and those who had remained faithful to him (a rapidly diminishing number in the post-war years) were for me creatures of legend who I could hardly believe still walked the earth. For another I had (and still to some extent have) a prejudice against planning ahead when visiting an unknown city. Afterwards I always regret it. My first visit to New York, for example, would have been much more enjoyable if I had taken advantage of the offers to pave my way.

The train, the boat, the train. Emerging from a tunnel, while passing through the excitingly 'foreign' yet familiar countryside, I had traced with my finger in the condensation on the carriage

window the name 'Max Ernst'. A young man seated opposite immediately told me that his mother owned several pictures by this artist and offered me his telephone number should I wish to see them. I took this as a promising example of the 'certainty of hazard', a theory Mesens had explained to me as central to Surrealist doctrine.

Arriving, wide-eyed, in the capital, I said goodbye to the young man who, his mother's Ernsts notwithstanding, seemed to me on the dull side, and took an extravagant taxi to Montmartre – I knew from E.L.T. that Breton lived there and that it had always been the centre of Surrealist activities, so I booked a room for a week in a squalid little hotel behind the Place Pigalle. During my stay certain evidence – a blonde hair on my pillow, the renewed ghosts of cheap scent and sweat every evening on my return, the interest the hotel owner expressed as to when I expected to be back – led me to conclude that during my absence it was available to whores and their clients, an idea which today, in more fastidious late middle age, I would find nauseating, but which at the time I welcomed as proof of that squalor I tended to equate with 'real life'.

Indeed, only half-an-hour later, swigging cheap wine and puffing on a gauloise, I was picked up by a not particularly attractive, ageing prostitute who suggested, after I had accepted her offer, that I also employ 'for only a few more francs' her 'sister' – who was, in fact, as my temptress was well aware, very much younger and more attractive. Before we set off I bought them both a drink, thereby foolishly allowing them a view of my still comparatively bulging wallet, and then we walked a short distance and booked in for an hour (this facility was not, I discovered, included in the fee) at a hotel almost identical to my own (had it been my room, the certainty of hazard would have been working overtime). Well this, I felt, was living. This: the sagging and squeaking brass bed, the damp-stained, peeling nineteenth-century wallpaper, the cracked bidet, confirmed everything I had expected from the films I'd seen at the Hampstead Everyman and the newly opened Academy in Oxford Street. After some mutual foreplay the older woman manoeuvred it in such a way (and with my willing compliance) that I found myself fucking the 'sister'. During this pleasurable activity some instinct, perhaps the fact she was holding my head as in a vice, warned me to break loose and look over my shoulder.

'The changing light of the arcades, a light ranging from the brightness of the tomb to the shadow of sensual pleasure.'
(LOUIS ARAGON 'PARIS PEASANT')
Passage Verdeau

'In vain, reason denounces to me the dictatorship of sensuality.'
(LOUIS ARAGON 'PARIS PEASANT')

Boulevard de Clichy
Boulevard Magenta
Café Le Palmier, one of several cafés in
the Place Blanche frequented by
André Breton

There I saw the other one, naked and ludicrously furtive, in the act of removing my wallet. I leapt off, retrieved it and asked her what she thought she was doing. She replied, with rather touching absurdity, that she was 'just looking for my photo as a souvenir'. Without comment I repossessed the still-intact wallet and concluded my transaction with it firmly grasped in my left hand. On my return to London, Mesens and his wife Sybil were very amused by my falling for the 'sisters' routine, apparently an old and famous trap sprung to impoverish the provincial or foreign visitor. E.L.T. added, however, that on one of his many early trips to Paris he had patronized two such prostitutes who had so fallen for him – 'I was very pretty in those days' – that they had offered him a position as their pimp. With implied nostalgic regret, he recounted that he had reluctantly turned down the offer and returned to Brussels.

As for myself, the girls said goodbye without any apparent rancour at their failure to rob me blind, and after a few more drinks in another bar with some swarthy young men who seemed perfectly agreeable to me buying them several rounds, I returned to my hotel. Checking my money I noted that, despite my lucky escape, I seemed to have spent a surprising amount. I had to be more careful if it was to last the week.

The next day I rang up the boy on the train who asked me on his mother's behalf to dinner, which surprised me because I had been told, and nothing since has disproved it, that the French will always meet you for a drink or take you to a restaurant but, on the whole, are reluctant to ask you into their homes. So that solved the dinner problem, and I spent the rest of the day going round the major museums including the Louvre where, rather shamefacedly, I sought out the *Mona Lisa*, justifying it to myself by imagining Duchamp's inked-in moustache and goatee beard, and Apollinaire having been accused of stealing it. I also had a disastrous lunch where I ordered artichoke and, never having eaten one before, tried to swallow the bristles under the contemptuous eye of a waiter.

The evening was, possibly due to my hopeless French, extremely boring, but I suspect it would have been so anyway. What I couldn't understand was why such banal people should

'The customers of this café are regulars whom I've watched, year after year, come in and sit down at the same place. There is absolutely nothing to distinguish them from the rest of mankind. What draws them here? ... For me, they are such natural phantoms that I scarcely notice them.'

(LOUIS ARAGON 'PARIS PEASANT')

Café Les Deux Magots, Boulevard Saint-Germain

The window of a retouching studio, Boulevard Bonne-Nouvelle

have hanging on their walls such beautiful Max Ernsts of the frottage period. It appeared that they were entirely uninterested in Surrealism and that included the mother who had bought the pictures in the first place. I would be less puzzled now. They were probably an investment.

The next day I made an appointment with Dr Mabille and in due course found myself sitting in his waiting room looking at some beautiful pictures by Wilfredo Lam. In my turn I was shown in by his receptionist and Mabille treated me rather as if I were a patient and Mesens' letter a diagnosis from a colleague. He confirmed all the other Surrealists were 'en vacances', and was perfectly friendly, but appeared rather perplexed as to why I had come to see him at all. He also made no suggestion that we meet again.

I spent the rest of the day going round the galleries on the Left Bank. Most of them were exhibiting painters like Pignon and Fougeron, 'modern' artists, supported by the French Communist Party and a long way 'after' Picasso or, worse still, Bernard Buffet's fashionable spiky sentimentalities, but the Galerie Maeght had a show of post-war Miró and, in the bookshop, quite a lot of current Surrealist literature, although naturally in French, and anyway I couldn't have afforded to buy it.

In the evening I went to a jazz club I'd been told about. The band played revivalist jazz heavily influenced by Bechet, and brusquely refused my offer to sit in, although I told them I was beginning to build a reputation in London. The audience, students dressed in black with white, expressionless faces which they believed to be 'existentialist', refused my friendly overtures with abrupt dismissiveness. Furthermore, the bill was enormous. I walked back to Montmartre, a considerable distance, in a state of depression and found I had already spent two-thirds of my allowance while not yet half-way through the week. Luckily, I had insisted on paying my hotel in advance and had a fat carnet of Métro tickets, but the prospect was bleak. Having seen Mabille, the only available Surrealist, I could have gone back to London next morning but pride prevented me. It was 'rotten herring' time.

So, for the rest of my time in Paris I walked, all day and often far into the night. I had no particular plan. I just let my feet carry me where they would.

Boulevard Saint-Germain

'The most vital images are the most fleeting.'
(ANDRÉ BRETON 'ODE À CHARLES FOURIER')
Café Glacier, near the Parc des Buttes-Chaumont

Square des Arts-et-Métiers

Bassin de la Villette

Lion de Belfort, Boulevard du Montparnasse

If I had taken a lot of money with me, or it had not been August and the Surrealists had been *in situ* and I had met them, I would no doubt have passed a more enjoyable week. I would have returned to London very full of myself, convinced that I was now a fully paid-up Surrealist who 'knew' Paris.

If I had read, as I have now read, a great deal of Surrealist literature, I could have at least planned an itinerary, visited, as I did on my last expedition, all the 'elective places', acted like an educated tourist in Greece or Italy, only with the Surrealist 'monuments' replacing the ruined temples or the pictures of Piero della Francesca. As it was, however, while knowing a considerable amount even then about the painters and their work, and having some grasp of the movement's aims and ethos, my only knowledge of the history of Surrealism was derived from the random memories of E.L.T. Mesens. In consequence, the sole 'monument' I knew about and went to look at was the Lion de Belfort, because it was the title of one of the collage 'novels' by Max Ernst which made up the boxed set *Une Semaine de bonté*, which I had pored over many times since I had acquired it some four years earlier when I was in the navy.

Carrying none of these aids, however, without defences, without aims, I was a true 'Paris Peasant', raw and open to every impression and close to hallucinatory through mounting and obstinate fatigue. By the end of the week I had begun to feel like a ghost, passing unseen through the animated crowds in the evenings, or along the empty streets in the small hours.

I had been bored, even on my first day, by the famous monuments: the Arc de Triomphe, Notre-Dame and especially the hideous and bulbous Sacré-Coeur (I made an exception for the Eiffel Tower). Soon, however, even those aspects of Paris that at first charmed me – the tall apartment houses with their balconies, familiar from the works of the Impressionists, the street accordionists, grinding out *Le Mer*, the berets, the smell of garlic and gauloises, the men carrying home long loaves of bread, the workmen still in their blue smocks, the shrugs, the still-extant *pissoirs* – became commonplace, unremarkable.

What emerged was a city in which the contrast between the great boulevards, the vast squares and enormous fountains and monuments, and the narrow, odoriferous warren of short streets tucked behind them implied a kind of architectural schizophrenia. Also, although I soon got to know the individual ambiance of a few districts – Montmartre, Saint-Germain, Montparnasse, Les Halles – once I had wandered off the beaten track, and especially in the 'outer boulevards', I had the sensation of being permanently lost as though in the desert, and half-expected to come upon my own footprints as though I had been walking in a circle.

The impression was heightened by the almost interchangeable cafés and the irregular but frequent recurrence of small shops which, because they sold the same product and for no other reason, displayed whatever it might be according to a rigid formula under a sign bearing identical typography and frequently reinforced by the same naive image: the carved equine heads outside the horse-butchers, for example. Many of the street names, too, seemed to me to act as mysterious signals beyond mere identification. The same was true of posters; but it was the statues that most impressed me. It was not just that there were so many of them – there are, after all, plenty in London – it was their placing. Some, of course, were sited in front of important buildings or around the edge of squares, but others were in such arbitrary positions as to suggest that they were human beings who had been ossified or caught unawares by the dust of a volcanic eruption.

Given that it was August, many of the shops were shut and there was a preponderance of tourists, but I gained some impression, especially in the less-fashionable districts, as to how public life appeared to be in such contrast to that in other cities I had visited. The streets, which in London are no more than a means of getting from point A to point B, seemed in Paris to be the place where life was lived, friendships and enmities forged, where lovers recognized each other at first sight. I was surprised too at the behaviour of those lovers: the way they froze in an intimate embrace as though in mutual solitude, something London was not to experience for well over a decade. The Parisian streets suggested momentous encounters although none – I was invisible, after all – came my way. On the other hand, private life appeared excessively private; one had none of those glimpses into rooms (the pouring of drinks, a quarrel) which interested me on my nocturnal walks through London. What windows there were opening on to the street were either heavily obscured by net or firmly shuttered. Doorways, some grand and ornate, some simple, let into sheltered courtyards. Life there

'The disembowelled horses
in the arena of heads.'
(TRISTAN TZARA 'LA BONNE HEURE')
Jardin des Tuileries
Rue Paradis

'Without the shadows, light could not ride the objects, and the sun would go everywhere on foot.'

(MALCOLM DE CHAZAL 'LE SENS PLASTIQUE')

Jardin des Plantes
Église de la Trinité

turned inwards, protected by the hawk-eyed *concierges* who Mesens always maintained were a source of great danger to the Resistance during the war.

For four days I did nothing extraordinary, had no overt adventures, but I was convinced, like a fisherman casting fruitlessly hour after hour across a river, that at any moment it would all happen: the line would tighten, the rod bend, the reel screech. To relieve my solitude I chose to people the streets with literary and artistic personages; perhaps Rimbaud and Verlaine quarrelled on this corner? Was it on this bridge that the young Picasso, at the time when Apollinaire came under suspicion of stealing the *Mona Lisa*, had thrown in panic those primitive statuettes purloined from the Louvre into the Seine? Was it here that Alfred Jarry ordered green ink to be brought to his table and then drank it? Did the Surrealists meet at this café in Montmartre or that one? I remarked too how the Art Nouveau entrances to the Métro resembled the chimeras of Ernst and Dali; only later did I discover that Dali had written at length in praise of Art Nouveau architecture, at that time despised, and had illustrated his article with a photograph of a Métro entrance. What I was doing, although I didn't know it, was using Surrealism to try and exorcise Surrealism; I was employing snippets of gossip or history derived from what I'd read or what E.L.T. had told me to hold at bay that 'Mystery and melancholy of the street' which lay at the very centre of Surrealist inspiration. Nevertheless, I was probably closer to the Surrealist spirit during those four days than at any time in my life.

On the last afternoon, for I was to catch an early-evening train, I discovered that, thanks to my strict regime, I had a little more money left than I had expected and decided to stand myself a Pernod (proof of my non-insular sophistication, I told myself) at the Café de Flor, and there, sitting at the next table, was the young Lucian Freud whom I not only knew in London, but who was actually under contract to the London Gallery. His greeting, characteristically casual and with the eyes seeming to pass through rather than to rest on the person he was addressing, restored me to myself. I was again someone who knew people, someone with a job, a family, a possible future in jazz. He told me that he had just bought, in the market, some tropical birds and, as his room was nearby, would I like to see them? I said of course I would; at that point I would have walked four

'Certain ones he licked, others he would never have dared touch, for
they were queens, truly regal in their personality.'

(LOUIS ARAGON 'PARIS PEASANT')

Porte Strasbourg, Jardin des Tuileries

'The terrifying and edible beauty of Art Nouveau architecture.'
(SALVADOR DALI 'MINOTAURE' 1933)
Porte Dauphine Métro station

A Métro ventilation shaft in the Boulevard Rochechouart

miles to examine a used pocket handkerchief; and anyway, Lucian has always had an ability, without seeming to imply that what he proposes is more than a casual and unimportant offer, to suggest that he is conferring a rare privilege. Chattering wildly after my long, involuntary silence, I followed him round the corner and up four flights of stairs. In his room were the promised birds crammed into a small but pretty wicker cage, and in the rather grubby bed a pale, wide-eyed and beautiful girl who, he explained, wasn't very well. I said hello, very impressed, not to say jealous, and duly admired the birds. Lucian later painted that girl in that bed with himself leaning with his back against the balcony. I saw it recently in the big retrospective at the Hayward; it shook the memory so vigorously that for a moment I was back in Paris on that hot, hazy afternoon some forty years ago. Not wanting to outstay my welcome, not knowing quite how I was expected to react to the sick waif – Lucian, as far as I can remember, behaved as if she wasn't there – I pretended I had something to do, and filled in the time until I was ready to catch my train.

When I got back to London I told everyone, perhaps even half-believed, that I'd had a marvellous trip. I told Mesens I'd seen Freud: 'I also', he said, 'I pointed him out to Breton last May as our most promising young painter and he asked me,' Breton was a notorious homophobe, '"Why then is he in the company of pederasts?"' I told my mother, simply to surprise and shock her, a deliberate lie, namely that I'd spent half the money she gave me on one meal in the best restaurant in Paris. I boasted in the jazz world of innumerable visits to whores of staggering beauty and deprecated, with some venom, the poor quality of French jazz. So one licks one's wounds.

But what I told nobody, and didn't, indeed, realize at the time, was how I had involuntarily paid my dues to the Surrealist spirit. I have returned many times over the years, with friends, with lovers, to write an article for *Vogue* on the Dali retrospective, to visit a terminally ill friend, to act a small part in a film set at the top of the Eiffel Tower. I eventually met Breton and attended a Surrealist *séance*, but as I have studied Surrealism I have come to realize that, due to circumstances not of my own making, that first visit was crucial to my understanding, a solitary initiation rite, a metamorphosis into 'the blind swimmer'.

'Life itself has summoned into being this poetic deity which thousands will pass blindly by, but which suddenly becomes palpable and terribly haunting for those who have at last caught a confused glimpse of it.'

(LOUIS ARAGON 'PARIS PEASANT')

Passage Reilhac

3

'Its fleece burns yet'

'It would be no exaggeration to say that Paris itself was one of the dominant influences on the evolution of Surrealist thought.' So wrote Roger Cardinal of the city's critical role in the development of Surrealism.

In their haphazard yet deliberate strolls through Paris the Surrealists, when in each other's company, were open to signs and portents concealed behind the banal surface of everyday life; but when they walked alone what they most hoped for was an amorous encounter spontaneously ignited by a glance charged with meaning exchanged across a crowded café or in the bustling streets. Of course, a purely commercial adventure in no way qualified in this context, or at any rate not in Breton's view.

That Paris should provide the setting for such adventures, whether hoped for or realized, was no coincidence. Paris for the Surrealists not only carried the promise of love, she was also herself a metaphorical woman. Cardinal puts it like this:

> Love is a major theme of the Surrealists, and much of their attention to the topic of Women is coloured by their parallel adoration of Paris . . . the Surrealist map of love is precisely the map of Paris, a street plan comprising irrational cross references and emotional index. At times the city at large submits to what Ferdinand Alquié calls 'Breton's feminised perception' and the latter's 'Pont Neuf' is a text based on the premise that the Île de la Cité, its bridges and the Seine, constitute an outstretched female body, complete with erogenous zones.

Of the river itself Breton writes, 'If for a second you attribute to the Seine the gesture of letting the arm she held bent against her forehead glide along her thigh like a woman', while of the Place Dauphine he insists, 'It is, make no mistake, the sex of Paris that

Île de la Cité

is stretched under its shadows. Its fleece burns yet.' This bold anatomical conclusion was inspired by the fact that the Place is a triangle, and the 'fleece' a twin row of trees which bisects it.

The only difficulty in this generally convincing metamorphosis of city into woman is the absurdly phallic Eiffel Tower, for many people the emblem of Paris. The Surrealists were not unaware of this problem. In one of their more or less light-hearted enquiries into 'the possibilities of the embellishment of the town' it was proposed that 'only the top half be left', a not-too-convincing proposal affecting little except the structure's *amour-propre*. A more radical and satisfactory solution is offered in a poem by Aragon, aptly entitled *The Transfiguration of Paris*:

> But the finest moment was when from between
> Its parted iron legs
> The Eiffel Tower let us see a female sex organ
> We scarcely suspected it had.

Other lesser phallic monuments were also chosen as candidates for modification in order to protect the femininity of the city. The Obelisk, for example, was to be moved to the entrance to the slaughter houses, 'where it will be held by an immense gloved hand'. This was Breton's suggestion, and it was he elsewhere who claimed to have had a vision of that same monument, *in situ* in the Place de la Concorde, being fellated by a kneeling and, in consequence, gigantic nude negress. He also proposed that the Vendôme column should be replaced by the statue of a woman climbing up a factory chimney. The trick, then, where there seemed to be no way of transforming a masculine structure into a feminine one, was to provide the potential provocation necessary for its eventual detumescence.

It seems to me, in examining these propositions, that the Surrealists were jealous of Paris. She was *their* mistress and they resented the threat of these examples of erectile architecture. In the case of the Vendôme column they had a further reason to detest it: its patriotic significance. Loathing *La Gloire* in all its forms, they proposed to smother the Arc de Triomphe in manure prior to blowing it up, and to surround the statue of Clemenceau with thousands of bronze sheep and one of camembert. (This image is more satiric than Surreal, perhaps. In the First World War some French troops, ordered over the top to

Place de la Concorde

Place Vendôme

The Eiffel Tower

face almost certain death, registered their feelings of outrage by baaing like sheep on the threshold of a slaughterhouse. The cheese sheep would, after a very short time, provide the appropriate stench.)

As for the law courts, Breton suggested razing them to the ground and tracing a 'magnificent graffito' on the site to be seen from the air. Paul Éluard wanted to replace them with a bathing pool. Benjamin Péret agreed, but proposed that it should admit only 'beautiful nude women'. Breton wanted to change the Opéra, symbol of official culture, into a foundation of perfumes and rebuild the staircase with the bones of prehistoric animals. Tristan Tzara preferred human skeletons replacing the exterior baroque decoration, and to rehouse inside that section of the zoo devoted to monkeys and kangaroos.

Religion, symbolized by Notre-Dame, got off less lightly. Breton wanted its towers replaced by 'an immense oil and vinegar cruet, one flask filled with blood, the other with sperm'. The building would be used as a school for the sexual education of virgins; a rather De Sadian notion that. Paul Éluard's solution for the Obelisk also involved a church. It was to be inserted delicately into the steeple of the Sainte-Chapelle. Thus the Surrealists suggested the destruction or transformation of the symbols of patriotism, the law, 'culture' and religion which they believed degraded, by their very existence, their beloved Paris, in order to restore the purity of 'the map of love'.

Naturally none of these alterations was carried through, nor did the Surrealists expect them to prove acceptable, on the contrary. However, suppose they had included the Louvre: perhaps one of them might have come up with, 'The present entrance to be suppressed in favour of a huge glass pyramid in the gardens'. This has, of course, recently become a reality, as has the erection outside the Saint-Lazare station of two towering columns by Arman, one of clock-faces all showing different times and pointing in different directions, the other a pile of suitcases. Not long ago a man walked down a tightrope from the top of the Eiffel Tower carrying a copy of *The Rights of Man* and placed the book in the hands of an official on the ground. This is not to suggest, however, that Surrealism has won, far from it, but merely that its superficial aspects have been absorbed by officialdom.

'What is that army of marine monsters swiftly cutting the waves? There are six; their fins are powerful and open up a way through the towering billows.'
(LAUTRÉAMONT 'LES CHANTS DE MALDOROR')

Rue Geoffroy-Saint-Hilaire

The Obelisk in the Place de la Concorde, seen from the Jardin des Tuileries

Notre-Dame

'The hands of the clock, pressed against one another and tired of waiting for the night, call in vain with a fateful cry.'

('LA RÉVOLUTION SURRÉALISTE')

Arman's column of clock-faces outside Gare Saint-Lazare
Contemporary sculpture by Pol Bury in the Jardin du Palais-Royal

'The eye has all the gestures of the fish.'

(MALCOLM DE CHAZAL 'LE SENS PLASTIQUE')

Passage Verdeau

Île Saint-Louis

But why, after all, was Paris the chosen city? Was it merely the coincidence of Breton and the others being there at the right time? Or a certain tradition of iconoclasm, of historical acts of revolt? Of anti-clericism? Of architecture, eroticism, the life of the streets? All these factors played their part, no doubt, and one must be aware, in retrospect, that what happened by chance may appear to have been inevitable, but even so the city connived and in part dictated the form in which Surrealism evolved. Its femininity acted as the ideal Surrealist muse; a role the movement assigned, much to the recent indignation of some women liberationists, to 'Woman' in general. No other city has this quality. Most cities are masculine.

The comparative failure of London to establish itself, despite the valiant efforts of E.L.T. Mesens, as a Surrealist centre is a case in point. No doubt there were many reasons: the absence of cafés (not at all a frivolous factor, as we shall see), the British mistrust of systems of thought ('Paul Nash', E.L.T. said, 'was a gentleman first, a Surrealist afterwards'), a lukewarm and short-lived commitment to group activity, a Protestant rather than a Catholic culture and so on, but even so the masculinity of London remains a major factor. It is a city with compensating features (although increasingly these are being eroded), but its charms are bluff, its vices oafish. In the nineteenth century, if Dickens is to be taken as evidence, there were still eddies and backwaters where mystery swam under the dark surface, but by the 'twenties and 'thirties these had been drained or diverted. Protected by the Channel, we remained obstinately insular and Surrealism, when it eventually arrived over ten years after its birth, was greeted with dismissive ennui by the majority of intellectuals, as a raree show by the public, and as a useful sauce to spice up their over-cooked imagery by those artists who were at a loss as to what to serve up next. With very few exceptions, nobody was prepared to face the splendours and miseries of living, or trying to live, the Surrealist life, and those who did, both then and later, came almost exclusively from the provinces.

It could be argued here, as I stressed earlier, that the same was true of most of the Parisian Surrealists, but for them the French capital distilled their efforts, sustained their beliefs and took them, whether as friend or foe, seriously. London never did that.

It was from Birmingham that Conroy Maddox and his friends, the Melville brothers, publicly refused to participate in the 1936 exhibition at the New Burlington Galleries on the grounds – which Mesens was later to agree were substantially correct – that many of the British exhibitors were in no way Surrealist. What happened was that Roland Penrose and Herbert Read raced hurriedly from studio to studio, searching for anyone whose work contained even an element of fantasy, and enlisted them on the spot. Eileen Agar, who at least has remained linked to the movement, described the arrival of the two recruiting sergeants who told her she was a Surrealist. 'Am I?', she asked. It is interesting to note in retrospect that Read and Penrose rejected the young Francis Bacon on the grounds that 'he was not Surrealist enough'!

Some of those they did choose left soon afterwards on honourable grounds. The great artist Edward Burra, most of whose work is radiant with the Surrealist spirit, quit because he 'didn't want to be told what to think, dearie'. Others drifted away for less creditable reasons. Henry Moore, whose early work was well within the canon, expelled himself by carving, towards the end of the war, a disgustingly sentimental *Madonna and Child* for a 'modern cleric' in Northampton. Surrealism, as a movement rather than a 'style', never really took root in London.

Elsewhere in Britain it was different. Like those seeds that establish themselves on the thread-thin fissures of abandoned industrial buildings, Surrealism, during the war and ever since, has lodged principally in provincial minds. Anthony Earnshaw, for example, a factory worker from Leeds, picked up on it and, 'while too shy to contact "real Surrealists" like Mesens', followed its precepts with remarkable perseverance and insight. He stumbled upon it in the late 'forties. His key, identical to my own as it happens, was Herbert Read's *Surrealism* – a book published some eight years previously by Faber & Faber in the aftermath of the London exhibition of 1936 and containing a long essay by Read himself, much of it somewhat irrelevantly concerned with the Romantic poets, but with many reproductions and contributions from Breton, Éluard and others. I can't speak for Earnshaw, but for me these essays and images, while inexplicable logically, suggested a world entirely marvellous and the antithesis of the grim reality of war and its peeling, dreary aftermath. As Earnshaw wrote in 1968,

It was in the late nineteen forties that, enamoured of Surrealism, I came to see my home city – Leeds – in a new light. Restless and not knowing what to do, I spent my Saturday evenings walking . . . seeking, I suppose, some avenue of astonishment. (Occasionally I was in the company of another but most frequently alone.)

These walks were in fact elaborate games. From some arbitrary starting point, I would walk to the other side of town using, as far as possible, only backstreets and side-roads – secret passages of yet another species.

Again, other evenings were spent tramriding, I boarded and alighted from trams at random for two or three hours. It was my custom to carry a book to read on these swaying, nocturnal journeys.

It was only later that I learnt that the [actual] Surrealists had engaged in very similar activities in Paris in the 1920s.

And so indeed they had; the haphazard and truncated visits to cinemas, for example, begun and terminated according to whim (a practice that would be ruinously expensive today); Leeds is a good city for such activities. For one thing, it is punctuated by magnificent nineteenth-century arcades, a preoccupation of the Surrealists, who prized them for their subterranean light in which one is not expected to linger. Earnshaw's instincts, later confirmed by knowledge, were sound. However, Leeds and other British provincial cities, while more conducive than London to the cultivation of the Surrealist spirit, were but a pale echo of Paris or, as Earnshaw formulated with precise black humour, 'For André Breton and his companions, Paris was a woman. It follows that *my* home city is a slatten. . . .'

The war dispersed many of the Surrealists and a considerable number, Breton and Ernst amongst them, landed up in New York, a city just as inhospitable to Surrealism as London, if for different reasons.

Initially, at any rate, there was a considerable effort to keep the Surrealist pot boiling amidst the skyscrapers and automats. The magazine *VVV* fulfilled the role of that succession of publications stretching back to the foundation of the movement in propagating its ideas and reproducing its artefacts. Peggy Guggenheim's gallery was largely Surrealist in its policy, many young painters, sculptors and writers were discovered and recruited; yet 'Surrealist' developments in America were rarely fired with a true Surrealist spirit.

65

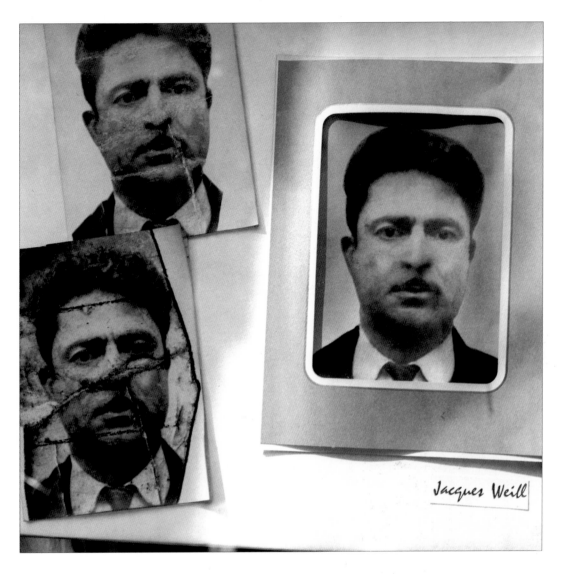

'Be careful, everything fades, everything vanishes. Something must remain of us . . .'

(ANDRÉ BRETON 'NADJA')

Retouching studio, Boulevard Bonne-Nouvelle

OVERLEAF

'The shadows take no notice of men's plans. They run off, and glide between the houses. Where do they come from? Shadows, shadows beware: you represent disorder and perdition.'

(LOUIS ARAGON 'THE LIBERTINE')

Passage Verdeau
Place des Vosges

Robert Motherwell, the Abstract-Expressionist, talked to me at some length about this comparative failure. To begin with, he pointed out, the arrival of Breton and the others was by no means the first exposure of Surrealism in America. Several private galleries had exhibited the painters almost from the movement's inception and as early as 1936 the Museum of Modern Art, New York, had mounted a huge exhibition, 'Fantastic Art, Dada, Surrealism'. Even so, the automatist strain in Surrealist painting, especially the work of Miró and André Masson, had certainly acted as an inspiration to his generation, although the story that Jackson Pollock started dripping paint through a punctured tin after a visit to Max Ernst, who had just invented that technique to register the flight of 'a non-Euclidian fly', is probably apocryphal.

Breton in New York was treated with respect rather than awe. Motherwell said that his tendency to arbitrate was the cause of some irritation: 'He would take a bunch of us round the junk shops on the lower East side, and demand we identify which objects were Surreal and which were not giving our reasons.' Motherwell also confirmed my belief that Surrealism flourished more vigorously in a predominantly Catholic culture: 'One time we had to make a list of our favourite myths and we [the Americans] all put down things like the unicorn whereas Breton's circle went for "the bloody nun" and so on. He gave us bad marks for that too.'

As in London, the lack of the café tradition was as much to blame as anything else. Max Ernst described the waning of Surrealist influence in the United States:

During my first months in New York there were many Paris painters here. At first the Surrealist groups seemed to have a real strength; but little by little they began to break up. It was hard to see one another in New York. The café life was lacking. In Paris at six o'clock any evening you knew on what café terraces you could find Giacometti or Éluard. Here you would have to 'phone and make an appointment in advance. And the pleasure of the meeting had worn off before it took place ... this situation cannot be changed. The Paris painters, when they arrived here first, tried to do so. But it is not enough for one person to decide, 'This is an artists' café'. Such a communal life as that of the Paris café is difficult – if not impossible here.

'What else remains but these cafés where we meet to drink these cool
beverages, these watery spirits.'
(ANDRÉ BRETON 'LES CHAMPS MAGNÉTIQUES')
Café Les Deux Magots, Boulevard Saint-Germain

Café Les Deux Magots, Boulevard Saint-Germain

*'In the vision that I have of the commander, it is a shoeshine parlour
that provides the site for his appointment with Don Juan, though
when the commander sat down beside him, the latter was already
losing himself in idle dreams. And smoking.'*

(LOUIS ARAGON 'PARIS PEASANT')

Flamingo Bar, Rue du Faubourg-Montmartre

Breton, in particular, without the café table to dominate, was like a pope in exile. His position was further reduced by his refusal to learn English – probably because, ever mindful of his dignity, he couldn't accept the idea of expressing himself clumsily or inadequately. Mesens told me with some scorn that Breton's own explanation when questioned on this point at their first meeting after the war was 'that he feared to adulterate the purity of his French'. For the leader of a movement committed to internationalism and opposed from its very beginnings to any form of chauvinism, it would appear a rather limp, not to say 'literary' excuse.

Breton was forced to earn his living in New York as an announcer on *The Voice of America* beamed at France. He had it written into his contract that the 'Marseillaise' was not to be played either before or after his broadcasts, but despite this concession to his loathing of patriotic symbols and despite his proven anti-fascism, it must have been hard for him to find himself voicing official propaganda, however 'pure' the French in which he expressed himself.

A further irritation must have been the way that Salvador Dali, now pro-Franco and reconciled with the Catholic Church, was considered to be Mr Surrealism as far as the American public was concerned. 'Avida Dollars' (Breton's anagram), aided by the disgusting Gala, used his undoubted genius for self-promotion to impose this concept. 'Fame is a job in New York' said Warhol later and Dali, who was in many ways a Warhol before the event, was proof that this was very much the case.

Then, as the war continued, many of the European Surrealists left New York to settle in more isolated and sympathetic American surroundings. Surrealism became a wan little ghost in the canyons of that dynamic, noisy and pushy city.

Breton himself escaped from it when and where he could. He was divorced from his wife Jacqueline, inspiration of *L'Amour Fou (Mad Love)*, and married Elisa Bindhoff who was to remain with him to the end. He lectured to the students of Yale, wrote some important poems (*Arcane 17, Ode à Charles Fourier*) and visited several Indian reservations in Arizona and New Mexico, but I believe that this austere and single-minded man, isolated by his refusal to learn English and out of sympathy with the confident materialism around him, yearned for Paris with every fibre of his being and in 1946, after a visit to Haiti en route, he returned there. He was home.

Haiti, where he attended a voodoo rite, was naturally sympathetic to Breton; one of those places he found 'Surrealist' in themselves. He had already, on a pre-war visit, declared Mexico the most Surrealist country in the world, and there were other places: Tenerife, for example, with its black sand and easily wounded cacti, which enchanted him. Indeed, most of the Surrealists travelled to renew their faith in the marvellous, or to recover from broken love affairs, and all of them left Paris every summer as a matter of course and frequently in each other's company. Nevertheless, they returned like migrating birds because Paris was for all of them, and for Breton especially, where their hearts lay. Other countries, other cities might be more overtly 'Surrealist', but nowhere else held in such balance the banal and the marvellous, the promise of the encounter with the certainty of hazard.

And so Breton returned. Sonia Orwell, George Orwell's widow, told me that she was there at the time and that when someone said 'Breton's back' a tremendous excitement overcame them all, even those, like herself, who in no way subscribed to Surrealism as a movement. It was taken as a certain proof that the war was really over and they hurried to the Café de Flor where he was sitting, surrounded by his friends, to reassure themselves that the great leonine head was indeed once again in their midst smoking its green pipe.

Yet, very soon, it was obvious that Breton was no longer at the centre of Parisian intellectual life. Surrealism appeared somehow irrelevant, frivolous and repetitive to those who had sat out the occupation, and Breton's absence was sensed, however illogically, to be a kind of betrayal. The bleak premises of existentialism seemed to fit the times and Sartre, as ugly as Breton was handsome, had assumed the role of guru. Éluard had deserted, like Aragon before him, to the Communists. Picasso also; 'Why does André never come to see me?' he asked Mesens with some naivety (or perhaps not). 'Engagement' replaced the pursuit of the marvellous. As history, Surrealism was admitted to have its place; even Sartre expressed his regret that he had 'not been through it', but it no longer seemed to provide any kind of answer to living in the post-war present in the shadow of the immediate and dreadful past.

4

'Who goes there?'

The three major works of Surrealist literature to which I have already referred several times not only demonstrate exactly what Cardinal has called 'The Surrealist perception of Paris', but were, in two cases at least, responsible for revealing and shaping the perception in the first place. The two earlier books, and the most rewarding, are *Paris Peasant* (1926) by Louis Aragon and *Nadja* (1928) by André Breton. The least satisfactory, in my view, is Breton's *Mad Love* (1937). The differences between them are particularly important, for the belief that Surrealism took an unchanging form is a delusion or malicious distortion that needs frequent correction. That it was initially the Surrealists' own fault is neither here nor there. Partly to blame for this distortion was Breton's early insistence on total automatism, a technique always suspect in the eyes of Aragon and eventually rejected by Breton himself. It is true that for those imbued with genius or even talent automatism did, initially, produce remarkable results. The trouble was that anyone could do it or fake it and if, in consequence, Lautréamont's dictum, 'Poetry must be made by all', appeared to be fulfilled, the results only too often were predictable, repetitive and increasingly self-defeating. This is not to say that automatism, when it insisted on taking over, didn't remain a source of the marvellous, but that as a *system* it led into a dead end, the prop room of a predictable theatre.

The vital link between the three books is the authors' evocation of Paris. In Aragon's case this presents no difficulty – it is the book's main theme. With Breton it is less simple. *Nadja* and *Mad Love* are both love stories; the former tragic, the latter triumphant. Yet Paris acts as far more than a convenient backdrop. Indeed, André Breton explicitly attacked the use, in novels, of 'realistic detail', the colour of the wallpaper for example, through which novelists hope to suspend disbelief. Paris,

'The mind spins like an angel, and our words are the small shot that kills the bird.'

('LA RÉVOLUTION SURRÉALISTE')
Rue de Turbigo

for Breton in both cases, is an active protagonist, a catalyst, almost a puppet-master. To emphasize its role as such is no more perverse than to place particular emphasis on the machinations of Iago in an analysis of *Othello*.

PARIS PEASANT

'Having observed', wrote Louis Aragon of his original purpose in writing this unique book, 'that all the mythologies of the past became transformed into novels as soon as people no longer believed in them, I formulated the idea of reversing the process and elaborating a novel that would present itself as a mythology.'

Aragon's quest for an effective modern myth was not uncommon amongst the Surrealists; it was, in effect, a central preoccupation. Max Ernst, for example, wrote of himself that, having died in 1914, he was resuscitated the day of the armistice as 'a young man who aspired to become a magician and discover the myths of his time'.

Aragon's solution to this problem was audacious in its apparent banality. Although topped and tailed by two ingenious and subtly anti-philosophical essays, attacking, amongst much else, our faith in reason alone as the only answer to any of the questions posed by the death of God, the main body of the book is made up of two long sections: the first devoted to a minute description of a double arcade which, even as he writes about it, is due for demolition; the second a nocturnal visit, in the company of André Breton and the Surrealist writer Marcel Noll, to a municipal park in the nineteenth arrondissement.

A threatened arcade and a public pleasure-ground may appear slender material for a full-length work. That, on the contrary, the book remains as mysterious, as elusive, as astonishing as ever, that it repays innumerable readings, is best explained by André Breton. In a generous description of his one-time friend and colleague some forty years after their final and irrevocable break, he wrote:

I still recall the extraordinary role that Aragon played in our daily strolls through Paris. The localities that we passed through in his

'The gateway to mystery swings open at the touch of human weakness and we have entered the realms of darkness.'

(LOUIS ARAGON 'PARIS PEASANT')
Passage Jouffroy

company, even the most colourless ones, were positively transformed by a spellbinding romantic inventiveness that never fal-
tered and that needed only a street-turning or a shop-window to
inspire a fresh outpouring.... No one could have been a more
astute detector of the unwonted in all its forms; no one else could
have been carried away by such intoxicating reveries about a sort
of secret life of the city.

It is exactly this 'outpouring', this 'romantic inventiveness' that
permeates *Paris Peasant*, which allows us, excluded as we are
from joining the young Surrealists on those enviable 'daily
strolls', to gather some idea of what they must have been like.

Yet, a modern myth? Those shops, hotels, cafés, hairdressers, small brothels, the stamp-dealer and shabby theatre,
which make up the double arcades of the Passage de l'Opéra are
of nineteenth-century origin, and down at heel; that suburban
park with its fake island looming up from an ornamental lake in
a district noted for its crime rate; neither of these evoke the
'twenties with their passion for speed, streamlining, the telephone, the skyscraper. It is, in fact, surprising how little modern
life impinged on the Surrealist imagination. Science and tech-
nology were alien to it. The cinema was welcomed, certainly,
but for the hypnagogic effect of its imagery alone. In general the
Surrealists chose to look backwards, over their shoulders. The
question is, why?

Breton was well aware of the problem. 'Human psychism', he
wrote, 'in its most universal aspect has found in the Gothic
castle and its accessories a point of fixation so precise that it
becomes essential to discover what would be the equivalent for
our own period. (Everything leads us to believe that there is no
question of it being a factory.)'

Some effort was made to fulfil this dictate. Even in *Paris
Peasant* Aragon speaks of 'great red gods, great yellow gods,
great green gods.... Painted brightly with English or invented
names, possessing just one long, supple arm, a luminous faceless
head, a single foot and a numbered wheel in the belly, the petrol
pumps sometimes take on the appearance of the divinities of
Egypt'. He maintains that their supplanting of traditional icons
is the outcome of speed. 'The folds of these Virgins' robes pre-
supposed a process of reflection wholly incompatible with today's principle of acceleration', but he doesn't go on for long in

this vein. The whole concept is, anyway, far more Futurist than Surrealist. Surrealism, Aragon maintained, is rooted in the nineteenth century. It is the child, however rebellious, of Victorian romanticism.

For us, almost at the end of the century, 1900 seems a very long time ago. This was not the case in the 'twenties when Surrealism was young. The movement was, in part at any rate, a revolt against 'the father', whether progenitive or spiritual. Armed, without his permission and against his intentions, with Freud's insights, the young poets and painters attacked everything their parents had stood for. They were abetted, of course, by the terrible evidence of the Great War, which had exposed as a cruel sham all those standards – God, patriotism, the family, universal progress – for which millions of young men had choked in mud or rotted on barbed wire, and yet the Surrealists remained ambivalent; Ernst's marvellous collage novels are acted out in stifling nineteenth-century interiors or gas-lit courts and alleys. Aragon himself asserted that 'a single step into the past is enough for me to discover the sensation of strangeness which filled me when I was a creature of pure wonder'. It was exactly those corners of Paris that defied progress which caught the Surrealists' imagination. That the Passage de l'Opéra trembled on the edge of destruction gave it additional layers of meaning and a particular poignancy.

'It is only today,' wrote Aragon, 'when the pickaxe menaces them [the arcades], that they have at last become the true sanctuaries of a cult of the ephemeral, the ghostly landscape of damnable pleasures and professions.' He added, with a certain gloomy relish, that these were 'Places that were incomprehensible yesterday, and that tomorrow will never know'.

Besides their imminent destruction, there was a further reason why Aragon was especially attracted by those particular arcades. That was the presence of the Café Certa, a place sanctified by the fact that, in 1919, Breton and Aragon had elected it as 'the rendezvous of friends', and which remained what the author calls 'the principal seat of Dada's assizes'. Aragon writes a panegyric on the subject of the Café Certa complaining, in that one has to complain about something in those circumstances, if only to throw one's praises into greater relief, about the way they served their coffee; 'I cannot help being filled with a sort of bemused sentimentality.'

81

Passage des Princes

You would imagine from this seductive description that Aragon was describing days long gone. In fact in 1924, when he began to write *Paris Peasant*, the ink was hardly dry on the first Surrealist Manifesto, and although Breton's war against those who had remained faithful to Dada was virtually won, there were still some pockets of resistance. This ability to turn yesterday into distant history and to speak of events that took place three hundred years before as if they had happened the previous evening, this bending of time, is very much a Surreal device. Still more relevant, although allied to this practice, was the determination of the Surrealists, from the very beginning of the movement, to perceive themselves as mythical beings whose least action, whether physical or mental, was already the stuff of legend.

There they were, in their twenties, unknown outside Parisian literary circles, and even there thought of as no more than talented punks who had betrayed 'literature' to gain notoriety, yet they described a visit to a café, a stroll to a bookshop as if it were of eternal significance. Breton was the master of this solemn self-aggrandizement; Aragon took some refuge behind an ironic stance; but the point is that it has worked. Today, even its enemies perceive Surrealism as an important contribution to twentieth-century sensibility. For those of us touched by its aspirations, it remains the prospectus to a kingdom still denied to us. Sometimes we catch a glimpse... especially in Paris.

Standing at the entrance to the Passage de l'Opéra, the young Aragon defines why the arcade is the ideal Surrealist hunting ground:

> How oddly this light suffuses the covered arcades which abound in Paris in the vicinity of the main boulevards and which are rather disturbingly named *passages*, as though no one had the right to linger for more than an instant in those sunless corridors. A glaucous gleam, seemingly filtered through deep water, with the special quality of pale brilliance of a leg revealed under a lifted skirt.

Passage du Caire

'The special quality of pale brilliance of a leg revealed under a lifted skirt.'
(LOUIS ARAGON 'PARIS PEASANT')

Galien et Hippocrate, Antiquités Médicales, Boulevard Saint-Germain
Boulevard Magenta

'So many women, in league with these arcades they stroll along, are content to be solely women.'

(LOUIS ARAGON 'PARIS PEASANT')

Passage Jouffroy

'I refuse to blush at my own hyperbolic terms: ideas, race, Napoleon, history, I.'

(LOUIS ARAGON 'THE LIBERTINE')

Passage Jouffroy
Passage Verdeau

It is not my intention to provide a précis of Aragon's marvellous book. It is available in both French and English, the latter brilliantly translated by Simon Watson Taylor. It is necessary, however, to list and in part illustrate the various devices he uses to mythologize the place. There is, for example, straightforward listing of the various establishments, as dry and factual as a survey. There is lively reportage, witty and intelligently speculative. Then there is delirium, the metamorphosis of the ordinary into the fabulous as if the author, unbeknown, had swallowed a hallucinogen. This doesn't happen often; Aragon is content in the main to probe and hint at the secrets of the passage, at the ecology of this reef, but just when the reader is most lulled and amused . . . .

Early on the author describes a shop selling canes and walking sticks, 'displayed so as to show both stems and handles to their best advantage'. Aragon lists their pommels, revealing that he is a master of the seductive ordering of images: 'ivory roses, dogs' heads with jewelled eyes, damascened semidarkness from Toledo, niello inlays of delicate sentimental foliage, cats, women, hooked beaks. . . .'

One evening he waits for a long time in a small restaurant for someone who doesn't turn up. Every quarter of an hour, out of embarrassment, he orders a drink. When eventually he emerges into the passage, the lights are all off, but in the case of the cane shop,

> I was astonished to see that its window was bathed in a greenish, almost submarine light, the source of which remained invisible. . . the noise whose low throbbing echoed back from the arched roof. . . the voice of the sea-shells that has never ceased to amaze poets and film-stars. The whole ocean in the Passage de l'Opéra. The canes floated gently like seaweed.

These phrases, wrenched out of context, can give only the first impression of the astonishing effect of the whole passage, but there is more to come.

> A human form was swimming among the various levels of the window display. Although not quite as tall as an average woman, she did not in the least give the impression of being a dwarf. Her smallness seemed, rather, to derive from distance, and yet the apparition was moving about just behind the windowpane.

A shop window in the Passage Jouffroy

At first believing her to be a siren, Aragon suddenly recognizes her as a German prostitute, the daughter of a Rhine hunting captain, with whom he had been infatuated. When he cries out, 'The Ideal', 'she turned a scared face towards me and stretched out her arms'. At this the whole window display is 'seized by a general convulsion', then the submarine light fades, the sound of the sea dies, the concierge shuffles along to close the grille, and tells the poet rather brusquely to be on his way. Next morning, everything in the window of the cane shop is as usual but, in a side window,

> A meerschaum [pipe] whose bowl depicted a siren, had broken, as though it had been condemned to be a target in some seedy shooting gallery at a fair. From the end of this pipe's illusionistic stem there still protruded the twin curve of a charming breast: a little white dust that had fallen on the silesia fabric of an umbrella testified to the erstwhile existence of a head crowned with flowing hair.

Logically, Aragon got drunk and hallucinated, but that is only the mechanism. The vision he describes is of astonishing precision. I must have read it a hundred times and it never fails to move or convince me.

And then, without any warning, he begins to discuss the commercial rapacity of the Boulevard Haussmann Building Society, the company about to demolish the passage and paying only the minimal compensation to those who earned their living within its twin arcades. Not only does the author analyse the methods and tricks of the Society, he also reproduces the indignant and pathetic protests in the shop windows, the local newspaper reports, the appeals. It's very touching, it succeeds in making the reader angry even after so long an interval, and is hardly Surrealist at all.

It is this uneasy and yet somehow inevitable swinging between the poles of reality and Surreality which gives the book its authority. Immediately after stating the case for the tenants, Aragon decides to 'put my microscope aside for the moment'. He complains of a headache, a failure to distinguish scale: 'a water jug and an inkwell remind me of Notre-Dame and the Morgue . . . my pen is a spike of fog'. And then suddenly there is death, a 'charming if slightly dusty child'. Indeed, what Aragon claims that he 'forgot to say' is that the Passage de l'Opéra is a 'big glass coffin', dedicated to death and love in equal measure.

And so, shop by shop, premises by premises, sometimes doubling back on his tracks to investigate more fully a particular institution, occasionally jumping ahead for the benefit of comparison or divergence, he slowly uncovers the secrets of those twin arcades, the Thermomètre and the Baromètre which, in tandem, comprised the Passage de l'Opéra and stand as a metaphor for Paris in all its absurdity and splendour.

There are, however, many diversions along the way. When Aragon is bored (or perhaps imagines we may be), he takes a little holiday. He may revert to Dada:

PESSIMISM – PESSIMIS – PESSIMI
PESSIM – PESSI – PESS
PES – PE – P – p. . . , nothing more.

There is a short play in the spirit of Alfred Jarry. There is an analysis of Surrealism as 'a plague', written with the icy apocalyptic frenzy of his hero Lautréamont.

Another device he uses to divert us is to reproduce, in the original variegated typography of old-fashioned advertisements, personal complaints and gripes, publicity of various sorts; always a rich source of 'mystery' for the Surrealists. He describes, for instance, 'a charming advertising cutout', visible from a certain table in a café, 'representing a dog saying hello to another dog, bearing the following legend':

BONJOUR CHER AMI!

Avez-vous pris
vos biscuits
MOLASSINE?

Similarly, he reprints the entire drinks list of the Café Certa including, for four francs, a cocktail named 'Dada', and another for three francs fifty called 'Pick me Hup' (sic). In describing such things the Surrealists were far closer to reality than those who strove for great literary effects, for 'simplicity'. Bombarded everywhere by verbal and visual information whether cajoling or threatening, we city-dwellers may choose to imagine ourselves impervious, concerned only with 'common sense',

93

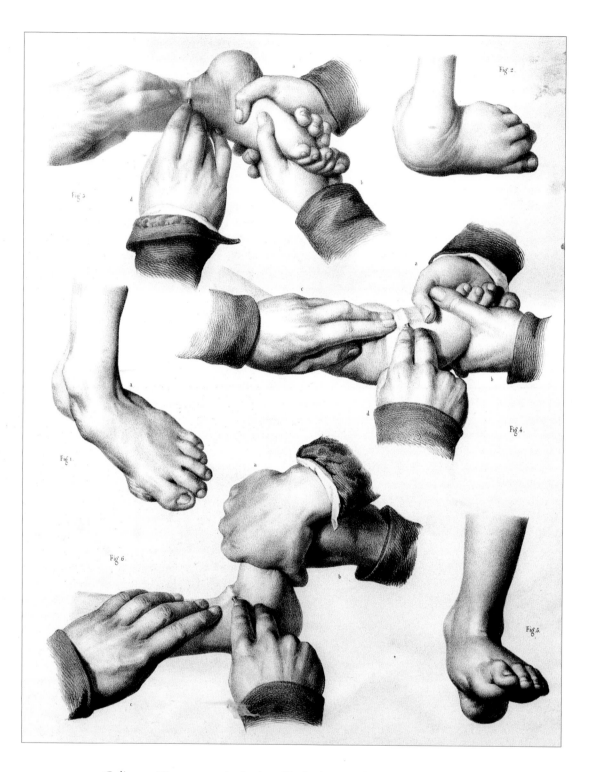

Galien et Hippocrate, Antiquités Médicales, Boulevard Saint-Germain

*'Ancient torture chambers lie dormant in the hydrotherapy equipment,
the electric massage equipment and under the lethal polishing.'*
(LOUIS ARAGON 'THE LIBERTINE')

A shop window in the Passage des Princes

with 'the job in hand'. The Surrealists knew better. Only James Joyce was their equal, and for very different reasons, in describing how we process this confusion, how it shapes our thoughts.

And always in the distance and growing ever closer comes the relentless demolition. The inhabitants of the Passage de l'Opéra busy themselves like doomed ants, but the spade is poised over their nest, the boiling water at the ready. The equation of love and death, that 'slightly dusty child', contributes to Aragon's effort to turn a novel into a myth. Most of the upper storeys above the shops of the arcade are rooms 'available by the hour', or modest brothels. Aragon, without illusion but with considerable harsh tenderness, contrasts the act of love, paid for certainly but none the less mysterious for that, with the greed of those speculators intent on destroying, for profit alone, its no-doubt squalid little shrines. The 'Passage' section of *Paris Peasant* is, in part, an elegy inspired by those modest whores he sometimes frequented. For one thing he attacks those who think of a brothel as 'a special kind of music hall to visit after an evening's drinking, in a gang', maintaining that he, on the contrary, found it 'inconceivable that anyone should visit a brothel except alone and in absolute gravity'.

The penultimate few pages of the 'Passage de l'Opéra' section are given up to a description of a visit to a small and shabby whorehouse in the Galerie du Baromètre. Most of it is written in exact, realistic prose; the decor described as precisely as the instructions, in old-fashioned plays, of what faces the spectator when the curtain rises. And the act? 'Come here, dear, and let me wash you. There's only cold water, I'm afraid. Sorry, that's how it is here.' And yet this 'realism' inspires Aragon to peaks of insight, lyricism and poetry.

No further use now for this language, this learning, this whole education through which I was taught to exert myself at the heart of the world. Mirage or mirror, a great enchantment glows in this darkness and leans against the door-jamb of ravages in the classic pose assumed by death immediately after shedding her shroud. O my image of bone, here I am: let everything finally decompose in the palace of illusions and silence.

And then, finally, a visit to the Théâtre Moderne, equally squalid and marvellous in Aragon's transforming eyes; a kind of strip-joint with a play as the pretext which has nevertheless given birth 'to an art as primary as that of the medieval Christian mystery-plays'. He quotes two lines from a song he hears there: 'This is the month of Venus. This is the loveliest month of all.' Banal? Not in this context – moving to the point of tears.

☆

The second, rather shorter section of *Paris Peasant*, while no less remarkable, is in an entirely different spirit. Its subtitle, 'A Feeling for Nature at the Buttes-Chaumont', is, I presume, ironic. The Buttes-Chaumont, a nineteenth-century park in a vaguely sinister inner suburb of Paris, is almost absurdly arti-ficial: its lake is pierced by a high rock resembling an island in a Chinese watercolour and crowned by a Greek belvedere, its paths orderly, its grass neatly mowed and enclosed by iron hoops. It is, in effect, the least 'natural' park I have ever visited. The 'island' is joined to the 'mainland' by a number of bridges, one of which was famous as a provocation to suicides but which, by 1924, was rendered less of a temptation by the construction of a little iron grille which Aragon calls a 'vertical extension of prudence', and which although 'easily negotiable' had entirely put an end to a 'practice that had reached epidemic proportions'. With its heritage of suicides, its artificiality, its sublime kitsch, the Buttes-Chaumont was very much an elected spot for the Surrealists. Was it sentimentality alone which moved me so much on my visit? At all events, I was touched partially by the sublime absurdity of the park itself, partially at the thought of those three young men, Breton, Aragon and the writer Marcel Noll who, on a spring night in 1924, decided out of boredom to take a taxi there from Montmartre to find out, although they very much doubted it, if it remained open; an expedition that was to form the reference point of 'A Feeling For Nature'.

Aragon doesn't describe their quest immediately. For several pages he explores, with a controlled lyricism and a profusion of startling images, his preoccupation with the laws of chance,

97

with religion and myth and, above all, 'nature' in its most arti-
ficial form: the invention of gardens. 'Not even', he writes of
mankind, 'when he started adorning himself with diamonds or
blowing into brass instruments did any stranger or more baffling idea occur to him.'

One evening then, overcome by boredom, the arch enemy of
Surrealism and, arguably, a principal factor in the invention of
the movement, Aragon decides to visit Breton in the Rue Fontaine. He arrives to find him surrounded by colleagues, all of
them plunged into a kind of stupor. To exorcise this Breton
suggests that he, Aragon and Noll set forth in search of adventure, but at first they are unable, like fractious children, to
decide what to do. They stop a taxi and Noll directs it to the Lion
de Belfort, only to be countermanded by Breton who changes
their destination to the park, although they all suspect – tension
is immediately present – that it will be shut. Noll, it transpires,
has never been there. The idea of the park 'stirred a mirage in
us'. There follows a passage of great beauty which, for me, sums
up the whole 'absurd', romantic, anti-rationalist and hopeful
emphasis of Surrealism.

> And so we began to think idly that there existed, perhaps, in Paris,
> south of the nineteenth arrondissement, a laboratory which,
> under cover of night, might correspond to the most confused
> elements of our invention. The taxi . . . was transporting us with
> the machinery of our dreams.

And then Aragon pulls a fast one. He describes the rest of the
journey with the precision of a manic travel guide – a device he
is to repeat later in his description of the layout of the park itself
– and so, in a thick fog, they arrive to find the gates open! 'We
enter the park feeling like conquerors and quite drunk with
open-mindedness.' And what takes place in the Buttes-
Chaumont? Nothing very much, but the effect is marvellous.
Night itself provokes an amazing reverie: 'The night of our
cities no longer resembles that howling of dogs of the Latin
shadows, or the wheeling bat of the Middle Ages, or that image
of sufferings which is the night of the Renaissance.' Modern
night, among a cluster of inspired metaphors, is seen as 'a
haunch of beef in the cities' golden fist'.

*'When we are moving, it is the tree
which becomes the spectator . . . .
The tree, having become a coffin,
disappears into the earth. And
when it is transformed into fire, it
vanishes into the air.'*

(RENÉ MAGRITTE)

Parc des Buttes-Chaumont

'The bridge trembles ... the bridge is in suspense .... Nothing could
be more gallant than a suspension bridge.'

(LOUIS ARAGON 'PARIS PEASANT')

Parc des Buttes-Chaumont

A statue speaks. What it says is not reassuring. The trio examine, by match-light, an absurd and touching monument erected by a Monsieur Eugo Payart, commercial traveller, with the assistance of a metal-founder, a cementer, a clockmaker, a manufacturer of Barometers (again!) and a manufacturer of gas apparatus. It lists, this four-sided column surmounted by a weathercock, the district's day nurseries, trade schools, streets, fire stations, casualty ward, and so on. (The column, according to Michael Woods, is no longer *in situ*. The authorities think it may be in a museum somewhere.) As in the case of the advertisements in the Passage de l'Opéra, Aragon reproduces the information in the varied typography of the original.

They ascend the bridge of suicides to the summit of the great artificial rock with its belvedere, they evoke a mysterious woman, the spirit of all women. They *see*!

In this remarkable chapter, which should of course be read in its entirety and of which, despite my best efforts, I have given no more than an ineffective précis, Aragon pursues a very different impression than that of the Passage de l'Opéra section. Human beings in the park are mere phantoms, a few students, lovers on benches. In the passage they are individuals full of quirks and gestures. Yet the combined effect of this two-pronged attack is miraculous: the city of Paris is held in its entirety as in a vice; the tremulous Surrealist spirit caught in a net of images. Despite Aragon's sarcastic denunciation of the whole book, his final, somewhat ambivalent, notes on metaphysics, despite his subsequent miserable embrace of Stalinist communism and the innumerable, long and extremely boring socialist-realist novels he wrote in its service, nothing can rob him of the glory of having written *Paris Peasant*. It remains a masterpiece. Perhaps, although Breton challenges it, *the* masterpiece of Surrealist literature.

E.L.T. Mesens, who wrote a poem denouncing the old bemedalled and painted Aragon, told me once how, during the early 'sixties, he saw him shuffling along the opposite pavement of a street in Paris, and was so moved by the memory of what he had been that he was almost impelled to cross over and embrace him. Even Breton in his last years softened enough to say a few words in admiration of his old companion. 'Sparkling' – yes. The only *mot juste*.

✫

'The great Suicides' bridge which, before metal grilles were erected along its sides, claimed victims even from among passers-by who had had no intention whatsoever of killing themselves but found themselves suddenly tempted by the abyss . . .'

(LOUIS ARAGON 'PARIS PEASANT')

Parc des Buttes-Chaumont

Parc Monceau

'Everything that is most eccentric in man, the gypsy in him, can
surely be summed up in these two syllables: garden. Not even when he
started adorning himself with diamonds or blowing into brass
instruments did any stranger or more baffling idea occur to him than
when he invented gardens.'

(LOUIS ARAGON 'PARIS PEASANT')

Jardin des Tuileries

NADJA

Breton's own books, *Nadja* and *Mad Love*, while equally evocative of Surrealist Paris, are entirely different from Aragon's. The most obvious aspect of this difference is that Aragon, while very much present in *Paris Peasant*, is capable of objectivity, whereas Breton is completely if magnificently egocentric. Indeed, the opening sentence of *Nadja* is 'Who am I?', and he goes on to refine this question by adding 'everything would amount to knowing whom I "haunt"'. Nothing in either of his books, not even the two women who engross and obsess him so profoundly, exists, except insofar as it has an effect on him. Paris itself acts as an extension of his own sensibility, treasured for the gifts it offers him. Had he been a bore, even a talented one, this self-obsession would have made him unreadable, but he is not a bore. His intelligence and sensibility, his sincere gravity, his painful honesty, are so overwhelming that we are prepared to yield to his spell. He is a true magus.

There are hints, nevertheless, that he was a little jealous of Aragon's earlier achievement. His suggestion, at one of the Surrealist meetings, that Aragon should read the first few chapters, all he had written at that time, provoked, as Breton must have expected, a storm of abuse. In *Nadja* too, after forming an acquaintance with a highly perceptive woman stall-holder in the flea market, that happy hunting ground, he cannot resist repeating her admission that she has been unable to finish *Paris Peasant*. Still, all this proves is that at times Breton could be jealous, a reassuring defect in his otherwise Olympian character.

There is another distinct difference between Aragon's novel and those of Breton. The former is able and willing to describe places and people objectively, with a considerable skill, and doesn't hesitate to do so. Breton, due consciously at any rate to his scorn for descriptive prose, rejects such 'effects'. To replace factual description he inserted into both his books a number of photographs, of places, people and works of art, and underneath them the relevant lines from the text. The effect is magical – especially in *Nadja* where the photographs are less 'glamorous', probably because they were taken seven years earlier – and adds a unique, poetic dimension. Nevertheless, even without the photographs, one would 'see' perfectly well. Breton's subjectivity, his moments of panic, exaltation, even his boredom, are enough.

The plot of *Nadja* is superficially simple. There are sixty pages, more than a third of the book, before the arrival of the heroine. They are devoted to writers he admires and to some aspects that touch him in writers he otherwise finds uninteresting. It describes how he meets, through a series of 'haphazard' coincidences, those who were to form the first Surrealist group. It reacquaints us with the Théâtre Moderne, but for him, unlike Aragon, it is a place of horror which he claims he frequented simply to learn a verse from a song. He describes too the full plot of what I suspect was an absurd play, *Les Détraquées*, which he saw several times at the Théâtre des Deux Masques; a melodrama set in a school where every year, during the visit of a mysterious Madame Solange, a pupil disappears and is later found murdered, and so hypnotic, so 'Surreal', is his exact description that this rigmarole holds us spellbound.

Above all though, during this long preface, we begin to learn how this man, to all appearances like other men, although extremely handsome, haunts and is haunted by Paris:

> Meanwhile, you can be sure of meeting me in Paris, of not spending more than three days without seeing me pass, toward the end of the afternoon, along the Boulevard Bonne-Nouvelle between the *Matin* printing office and the Boulevard de Strasbourg. I don't know why it should be precisely here that my feet take me, here that I almost invariably go without specific purpose, without anything to induce me but this obscure clue: namely that it (?) will happen here. I cannot see, as I hurry along, what could constitute for me, even without my knowing it, a magnetic pole in either space or time. No: not even the extremely handsome, extremely useless Porte Saint-Denis.

A little later there is a photograph of the arch, and beneath it the repeated words, 'No: not even the extremely handsome, extremely useless Porte Saint-Denis.' We are in his grip. I have recently and quite deliberately walked along the Boulevard Bonne-Nouvelle 'toward the end of the afternoon'. I would not have been surprised, although he has been dead now for almost three decades, to have encountered André Breton.

☆

Re-reading this last sentence at nine o'clock in the morning (it was written late at night after drinking brandy), I realize it to be nonsense. I would have been not only 'surprised' but flabbergasted. Breton, like Banquo, is in his grave, but it is nevertheless more than a simple and partially drunken literary conceit. While reading *Nadja*, for all its equivocations and literary flourishes, disbelief *is* suspended. The events described seem more than 'literature'. The meeting of Breton and Nadja, their temporary convergence, convinces the reader every time he opens the book and, like ghosts, they re-enact their tragedy – her madness, his eventual failure of nerve – over and over again. To claim that I would not have been surprised to have seen Breton in the Boulevard Bonne-Nouvelle is absurd, but equally it is impossible not to imagine him there taking his late-afternoon walk.

Places in Paris against which the book unfolds:

The Place du Panthéon
The Place Maubert (statue of Étienne Dolet)
The Carrefour Médicis
The Boulevard Bonne-Nouvelle
The Porte Saint-Denis
The Passage de l'Opéra
The Saint-Ouen flea market
The Rue Lafayette and an unknown intersection
(where he first met Nadja)
The Boulevard Magenta
(where she claims to be going to the hairdressers)
The Gare du Nord
Rue du Faubourg-Poissonnière
The corner of the Rue Lafayette and the above
The Théâtre des Arts
The Île Saint-Louis
The Place Dauphine
The Palais de Justice
The Louvre
The Tuileries
The Rue Saint-Honoré

Porte Saint-Denis

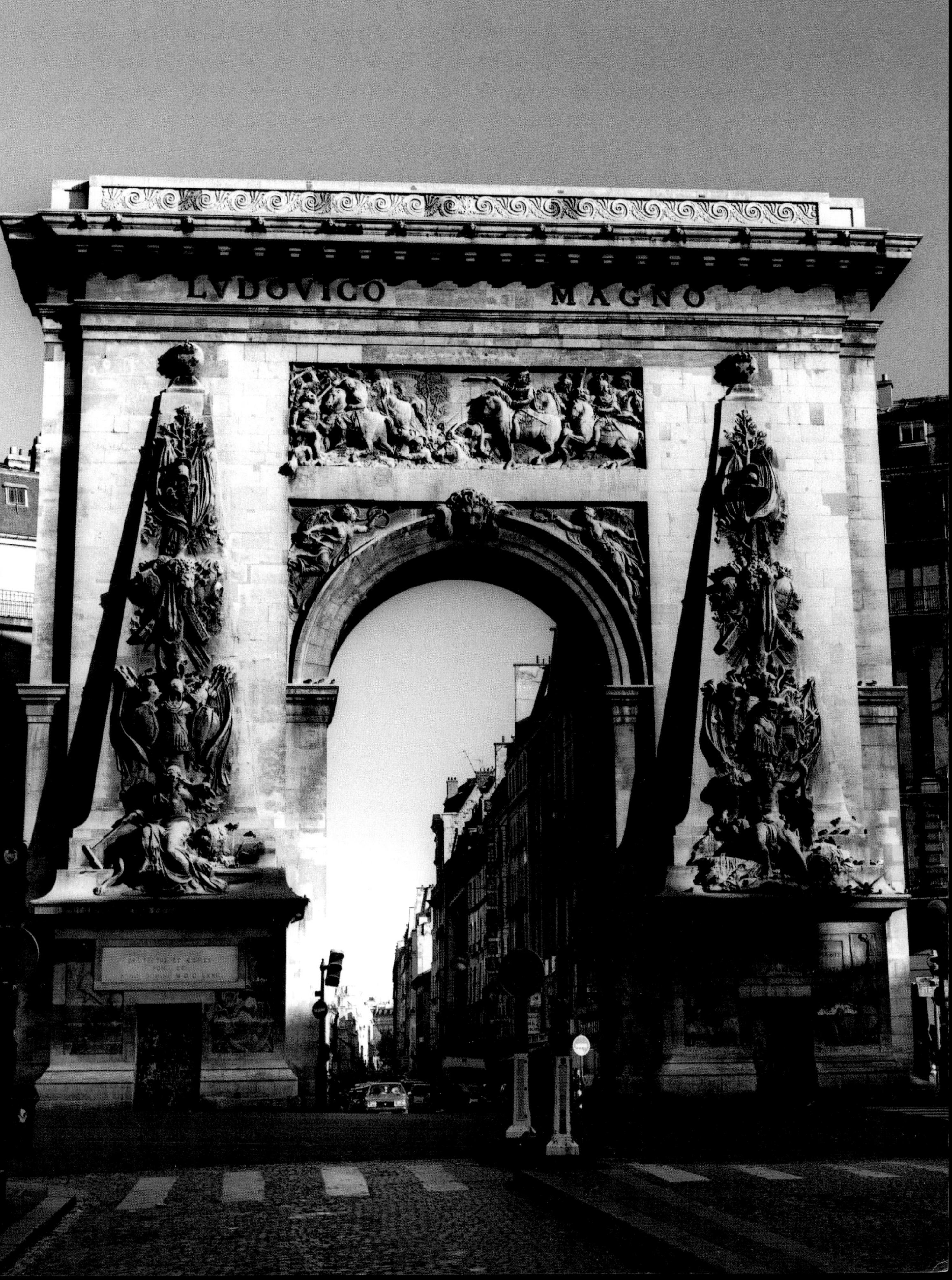
LVDOVICO MAGNO

The corner of Saint-Georges
The Rue de Chéroy
The Quai Malaquais (the clumsy waiter)
Le Peletier Métro station
The Rue de Seine
The Palais-Royal
The Rue de Varenne
The Boulevard des Batignolles
The Gare Saint-Lazare
The Rue Fontaine (where Breton lived for most of his life)
And many theatres, cafés, hotels, shops, and a waxworks

It would be possible, adding, indeed, a few places near Paris to which Breton and Nadja made excursions, to arrange a *Nadja* guided tour, rather as in Dublin you can visit the principal route taken by Bloom and Stephen in *Ulysses*. Possible, but not very profitable. The sites in *Nadja* should be visited, in the manner of Aragon patronizing a brothel, 'alone and in absolute gravity'.

✫

For Breton the importance of Nadja, the person not the book, was that of a muse. Someone who because of her nature, her 'madness', was able to demonstrate how 'reality', far from being concrete and measurable, can be shifted, become transparent, forced to reveal inconsistencies, become Surreal. Of course, before he met her, Breton and his colleagues had achieved this from time to time, or discovered in books and certain elected works of art, in the detritus that finished up in the flea market, evidence that it was possible. So too had Aragon's discovery that the hotel sign 'Maison Rouge' seen from a certain angle became 'Police', an illusion reinforced by a lady who had earlier offered the Surrealists one of her sky-blue gloves, and later that day taken Breton to see a picture with a surface of tiny vertical bands which, head on, represented a tiger, viewed from one side a vase and from the other an angel. Automatism and trance could also sabotage 'good sense', and so on, but Nadja didn't just provide clues. She offered a revelation of Surrealism constantly at full throttle.

Théâtre Grévin

'We, who speak with the sky, we, covered with dew, the mineral
dancers feared by the nights, we the tamers of breezes, the charmers
of birds, the guardians of silence.'

(LOUIS ARAGON 'PARIS PEASANT')

Parc Monceau

*'Our cities are peopled with unrecognized sphinxes which will never
stop the passing dreamer and ask him mortal questions.'*
(LOUIS ARAGON 'PARIS PEASANT')
Parc Monceau

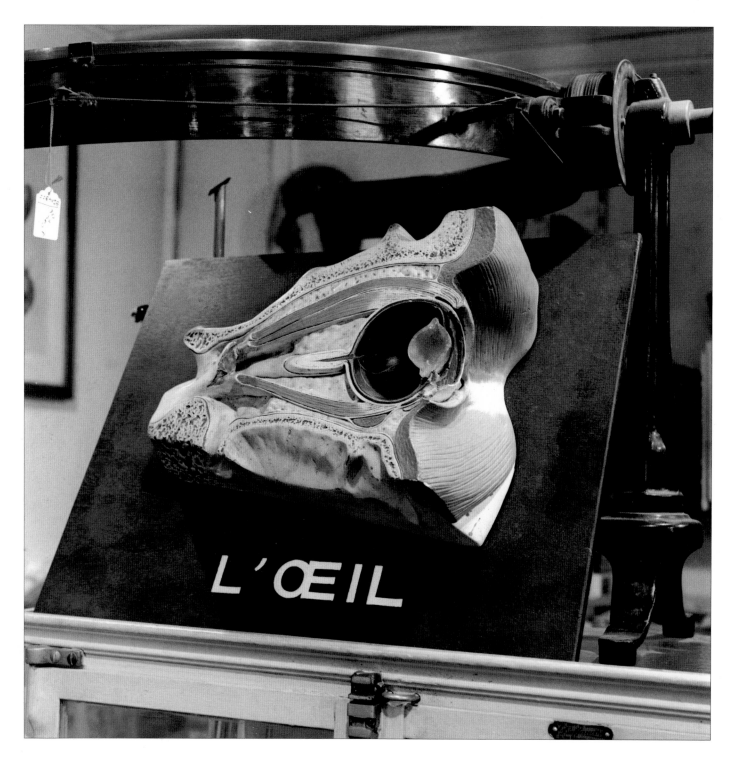

Galien et Hippocrate, Antiquités Médicales, Boulevard Saint-Germain

*'Meanwhile, you can be sure of meeting me in Paris, of not spending
more than three days without seeing me pass, toward the end of the
afternoon, along the Boulevard Bonne-Nouvelle.'*

(ANDRÉ BRETON 'NADJA')

Boulevard Bonne-Nouvelle

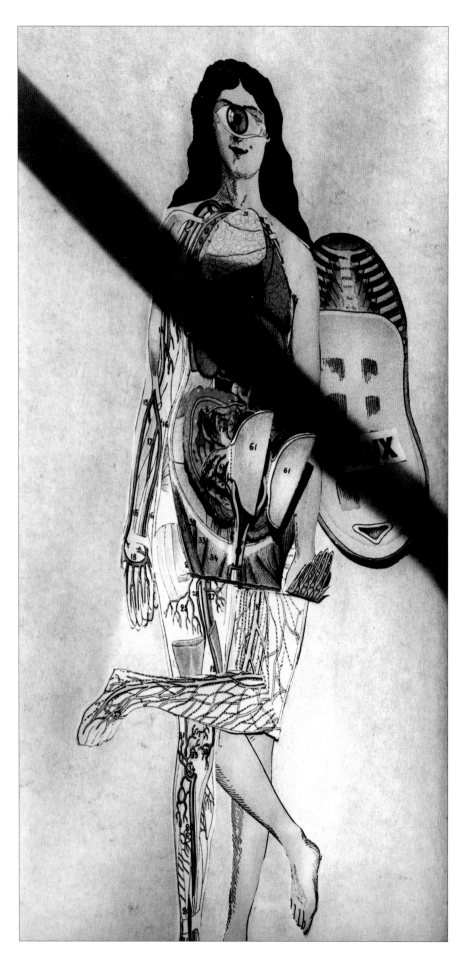

*'What you were running away from
You could lose it only in the arms
    of chance
That makes the ending of Paris
    afternoons so
fluctuant around the woman with the
    mad crystal eyes.'*
(ANDRÉ BRETON 'VIOLETTE NOZIÈRES')

Boulevard Saint-Germain
Saint-Ouen flea market

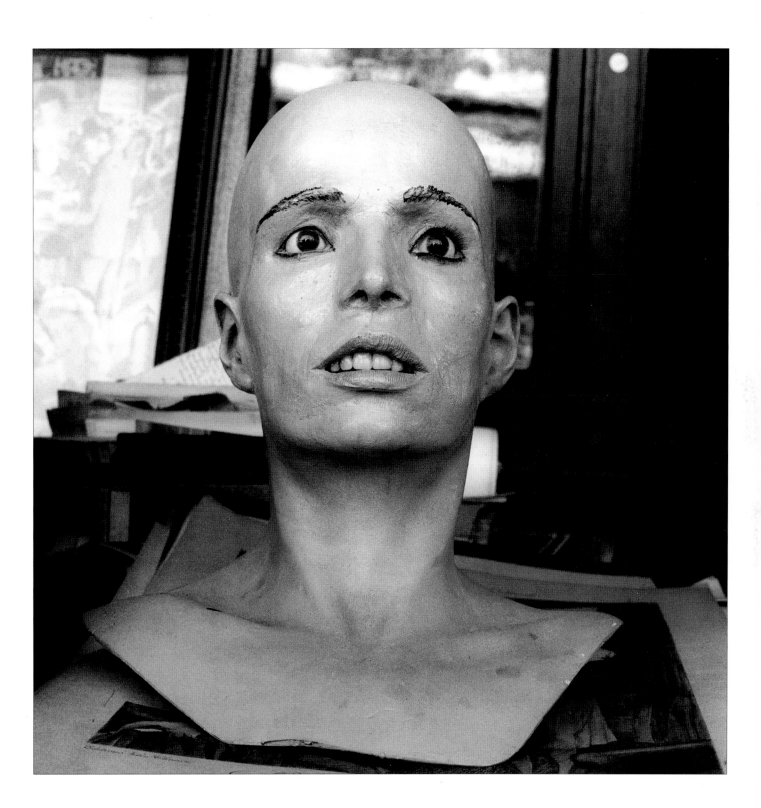

The pity of it, the tragedy even, was that the price she paid for this vision was an inability to live life by the rules. Breton realized this, quoting as an example how he and his friends would judiciously stand up when a flag passed, signalling their revolt simply by not saluting. Nadja would not, could not, 'stand up'. She lived – how? By prostitution mainly, a shift detested by Breton; while he appeared to accept that, for Aragon, prostitution encompassed a certain heroic pathos, Breton himself refused to believe that it could offer any kind of erotic solution. In consequence, he made this self-inflicted degradation unnecessary (or did he?) by supporting her during their liaison, although he himself was by no means well off at that period.

Nadja's other defect, from a practical point of view, was her inability to suppress anything. This eventually so depressed and occasionally enraged Breton that he stopped seeing her. For example, shortly before they broke up she described an incident where, in a restaurant, she refused to go to bed with a man 'because he was low'. He hit her and she called for help but made sure, before he was led away, that she bled all over his clothes. Breton, repelled by this story, realized the end was coming. He wept and couldn't stop. He was appalled too when he discovered that one of her lovers was a judge, detested by the Surrealists even more than most judges, on account of a callous and disgusting remark he addressed to a woman who had murdered her lover, saying that she did not even have 'the gratitude of her own womb (laughter)'. Then there were times when she became banal, flirtatious, and irritated him in consequence.

But finally, although here I risk the angry reproach of Breton's shade, madness in another is draining and exhausting, eventually insupportable, and Nadja *was* mad. The Surrealists courted and at times envied madness. They hunted it like Carroll's snark, aware too that, if they found it, it could turn out to be a 'Boojum'. Antonin Artaud went mad, Leonora Carrington was incarcerated, several others had temporary breakdowns, there were even a number of suicides, but in general most of them lived up to Dali's famous dictum, 'The only difference between myself and a mad man is that I am not mad'. Of course, the compensation for madness (for others, not for the mad person themself who is almost invariably frightened and miserable) is exactly what Nadja offered Breton – marvellous perceptions, hallucinations taken as real, poetic ideas – but the price of this perception is eventually too high. I once spent two days trying to persuade a friend of mine, a writer who had gone mad, to come with me to an asylum which I knew to be, in so far as any asylum can be sympathetic, the best bet. During this fruitless exercise he relayed the most extraordinary and convincing messages. Nothing could stop the flow of poetic correspondences, and the result? My total despair and exhaustion. Eventually, to my relief, he left me, believing me to be a Martian only pretending to be me. Two or three days later he was sectioned into the worst 'bin' in London.

But then he was simply a friend, not even a particularly close one. Breton and Nadja were lovers. Here too, though, lies the principal difficulty. Nadja loved Breton totally. She worshipped him. Breton finally, in self-preservation perhaps, didn't love her.

'I was told', he writes towards the end of the book, 'that Nadja was mad'. And what does he do about it? Nothing. He rails at psychiatrists. He points out that if she were rich Nadja's life in an asylum would be bearable. He claims, with some justice, that the company of others, all of them disturbed, often turns a crisis into a permanent condition, but he does nothing, and finally this is perfectly understandable and his honesty in admitting it even admirable. However, as a Surrealist it is a black, if self-awarded, mark.

The flavour of *Nadja* is perhaps best conveyed by Breton's account, here paraphrased, of an evening they spent together.

She believes she has ordered a taxi to take them to the Île Saint-Louis, instead she has given as their destination the Place Dauphine; an important if disturbing spot for Breton. At dinner that night, outside a café, a drunk constantly circles the table shouting incoherent obscenities (this ability of Nadja to provoke strangers is constant; later, during another dinner at the Restaurant Delaborde, a waiter 'fusses needlessly round our table, brushing imaginary crumbs from the cloth', and during the course of the meal he breaks *eleven* plates). At the conclusion of their meal Nadja maintains there is a secret passage under their feet. She also points out a window, 'black, like all the rest', claiming that in a minute it will light up, and will be red. A minute later it lights up. It has red curtains.

On a subsequent walk she has an attack of what seems to be agoraphobia. Looking at the Seine she sees a red hand: 'why is that hand flaming over the water?'

At midnight, in the Tuileries, watching the jet of a fountain, she interprets it: 'Those are your thoughts and mine. Look where they all start from, how high they reach, and then how it's still prettier when they fall back. And then they dissolve immediately, driven back up with the same strength, then there's that broken spurt again, that fall … and so on indefinitely.' Breton is astounded by this notion. It is identical to a description of a fountain in a book he has just finished: the third of Berkeley's *Dialogues between Hylas and Philonous*, in the 1750 edition, a work it is inconceivable she could have read. She doesn't listen to him, by now obsessed by the roaming presence of a man she believes once asked her to marry him. They head for a bar in the Rue Saint-Honoré called Le Dauphin. Nadja, of course, points out that they have come from the Place Dauphine to the Dauphin. She won't stay in the bar because she 'cannot endure the sight of a mosaic strip extending from the counter across the floor'. And this all in one evening.

Throughout the book Breton bumps into Nadja unexpectedly, but frequently fails to meet her, for one reason or another, 'by appointment'.

In a bar, the Régence, there is a peddler of cheap historical prints, one of which shows incidents from the reigns of Louis VI and Louis VII, a period in which Breton has recently become interested. The old man offers 'extremely confused commentaries' for the illustrations and, on receiving four francs (two of them a bribe to get him to leave), insists on giving them not only *all* his prints, but ten colour postcards of women.

Later Nadja sees again the hand tracing a line across the sky over the Seine, and a short time afterwards they come upon a red hand on an advertisement, its index finger pointing. Nadja insists on touching it. To do this she has to jump in the air several times before slapping it successfully with her own.

She then tells Breton he must write a novel about her; the one incident in the whole book that, for some reason, I doubt.

Place du Châtelet
OVERLEAF The Seine seen from Pont au Change

'Only someone quite devoid of feverish passion could enter a bathhouse without becoming immediately convinced that he is entering the heart of an enigma!'
(LOUIS ARAGON 'PARIS PEASANT')

Place Saint-Michel
Rue Geoffroy-Saint-Hilaire
Rue du Faubourg Montmartre

Pont Neuf

Place Dauphine

On a train one night, en route to Saint-Germain, they are kissing and she suddenly screams. She claims to have seen a head of a man wearing a cap, upside down at the top of the window. Breton doubts her but, leaning out of the window he indeed spots a railway employee, in a cap on the roof of the compartment. At the next station Nadja stands at the window and three men, in succession, blow her kisses.

These are actual incidents imposed on the real world, but of course there is much more: her poorly executed if remarkable drawings, her extraordinary statements, her ability to formulate an idea later confirmed from another source. Her interpretation of a painting by Max Ernst almost identical to his own written on the back of the canvas. Incidentally, Breton had asked Ernst to paint Nadja's portrait, but he had refused on the advice of a clairvoyant, and there is, indeed, no image of her. We know she has remarkable eyes, beautiful teeth, is blonde and very frail, but nothing else. We know her gestures but have no real idea of her appearance. She is a ghost. *Nadja* is a troubling and troubled masterpiece. Paris, for those who have read this book, is still haunted by her, by that 'forever pathetic cry':

Who goes there? Is it you, Nadja? Is it true that the beyond, that everything beyond is here in this life? I can't hear you. Who goes there? Is it only me? Is it myself?

MAD LOVE

The last of the three 'novels' in which Paris plays a major role is *Mad Love*. This contains some of Breton's most beautiful imagery and perceptions, and yet I have always found it, as a whole, the least interesting.

Trying to analyse why, I have reached the conclusion that it is partially to do with the date. By 1937, when it was first published, Surrealism and the Surrealist methods were completely established. The public, however superficially or mockingly, was well aware of it. Instead of the early and deliberately

A bookstall, Quai de Montebello

drab little magazines, its platform was now *Minotaure*, the Surreal 'glossy'. Its imagery, admittedly to the irritation and opposition of its originators, had been taken over by advertising, film and fashion. People felt they knew what to expect of it. With *Paris Peasant* and *Nadja* the effect, even to their authors, must have been astonishing revelation. *Mad Love* is, by comparison, predictable.

There are many parallels with *Nadja*. The opening section with its general probing into the revenge of the imagination on reason, its renewed demonstrations of chance, even a return, a very fruitful one, to the flea market follows much the same plan. There is the same resort to photographs, but many more of them are of works of art and objects trouvés rather than places or people and, especially in the case of those taken by Man Ray, they are in themselves less matter of fact, more beautiful, and in consequence less convincing.

More than all this, however, *Mad Love* moves me so much less than *Nadja* because it is written with someone else in mind, namely its heroine, Jacqueline Lamba, a professional exhibition swimmer, who was to become Breton's second wife and the mother of his only child. Everyone I have spoken to who knew her, everything written about her, suggests that she was (indeed still is) a beautiful and intelligent woman. Her photographs would seem to confirm this. Nevertheless, Breton must have written most of this book (the first section was completed before he met her) knowing that she would read it.

As for Nadja, locked up no one knew where, her removal allowed him total freedom to write what he chose; she had now completed her role. Jacqueline, on the other hand, was still part of his life, and domestic life at that. Most of the book is a love letter.

There are even moments, especially the final chapter written to his infant daughter Aube, when it becomes *almost* sentimental; no, it is sentimental, particularly in view of the fact that that undisciplined child was allowed, in the name of freedom, to terrorize those at the café table by, in Mesens' words, 'hitting us on the head wiz breads'.

It begins marvellously with an evocation of several men 'dressed in black – probably in full dress; their faces escape me ... seated next to each other on a bench, talking among themselves, always looking straight ahead'. A little later there is a similar number of women, also seated on a bench; the effect is Delvaux-like. 'A man enters . . . and recognizes them . . . . They are the women he has loved, who have loved him, some for years, others for one day.' Then all the men, and presumably Breton himself, sit facing the women, who share 'one face only: the last face loved'. *— individuals insignificant. love — is the only face remembered. have not individuals*

I have very much simplified the doubts and certainties that swim around and across these subtle and at times self-castigating few pages. What I believe Breton is trying to do is to reconcile somehow his belief in 'mad' love with his own inability to sustain it in life, with his first wife and Nadja both gone. Even his subsequent relationship with Blanche Derval has by this time faded too. What is it that goes wrong every time? He detests, indeed, rages against, those who take the pragmatic and cynical view that love can never last, that once the physical narcotic of sex loses its potency it's all over, leaving at best good-natured habit. Yet he too, it seems, is unable to sustain love. The men who are one man, the women who are one woman, are his attempt to tease out a solution (one doesn't have to be Breton, of course, to come to the conclusion that all those we love, in retrospect at any rate, have much in common). *'love' transient. never had sex with Nadja. — did he love her (see notes) Nadja.*

There follow typical and brilliant thoughts on poetry, chance, the qualities of crystal, and the eventual visit to the flea market. Here his companion Giacometti discovers a metal mask, original use unknown, which helps him to solve the problem of the face of a sculpture he is working on, and Breton a large wooden spoon of peasant origin whose handle rests on a little shoe. During the purchase of these objects they are, unbeknown to themselves, watched by two witnesses, one of whom turns out to be Blanche Derval herself, with whom Breton has long lost contact, and who had almost bought the mask herself, but was too disturbed by its aura. Not without reason. Later on, when a photograph of the mask was published in a Belgian magazine, Breton received a letter from Joe Bousquet, a brilliant Surrealist writer, paralysed and bedridden as a legacy of the Great War. Apparently the mask was 'one of those he had to hand out to his company . . . just before the attack in which a great number of his men were to die and he was himself to get the bullet in his spine which immobilized him'. Furthermore, he insisted 'on the evil role of this mask, not only illusory in its protection, but even awkward, heavy, distracting, *coming from*

131

*'The objects that . . . go off to dream at the antique fair had been just
barely distinguishable from each other . . . . They flowed by, without
accident, nourishing the meditation that this place arouses,
concerning the precarious fate of so many little human constructions.'*

(ANDRÉ BRETON 'MAD LOVE')

The Saint-Ouen flea market

another epoch, and which had to be abandoned after this experience'. This terrible coincidence and the unseen presence of Blanche Derval indicate that that day the certainty of hazard at its most sinister was hard at work.

After discussing with Éluard the mask, its frightful secret, his ex-mistress as an unseen witness, and equating all these factors with Freud's views on the twin functions of our instincts for death and sex – the mask and the spoon – Breton finally declares himself open to what may come. 'But I had to start loving again, not just to keep on living!'

In a certain café, for two evenings running, Breton had noticed and been excited by a very beautiful woman – '*scandalously* beautiful' he describes her later – sitting writing alone and whose fate, he tentatively believes, 'could some day ... be entwined' with his. His description of her complexion appears to me to be an example of late Surrealism at its most overheated and baroque:

> Imagined in perfect concord between rust and green: ancient Egypt, a tiny, unforgettable fern climbing the inside wall of an ancient well, the deepest, most sombre, and most extensive of all those that I have ever leaned over, in the ruins of Villeneuve-lès-Avignon, a splendid fourteenth-century French town today abandoned to gypsies.

Compare this with his initial description of Nadja, so simple and mysterious, vague even, and yet, in my view, so much more *Surreal*:

> Suddenly, perhaps still ten feet away, I saw a young, poorly dressed woman walking toward me, she had noticed me too, or perhaps had been watching me for several moments. She carried her head high, unlike everyone else on the sidewalk. And she looked so delicate she scarcely seemed to touch the ground as she walked. A faint smile may have been wandering across her face.

Roger Cardinal, in his rather stern critique of *Nadja*, reproaches Breton for that 'may have been' smile. Either she was smiling, he writes, or she wasn't; but for me, although he is logically correct, the sudden loss of memory on this point is very touching, much more so than all that peering into wells, however deep and sombre.

133

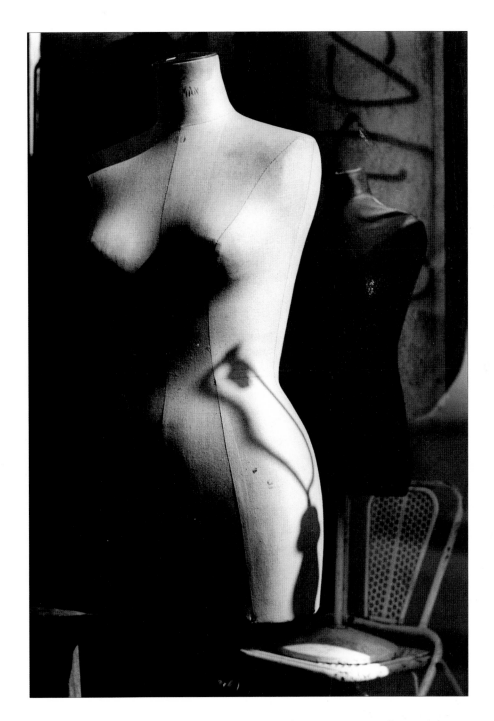

'Marcel Noll and I went one Sunday to the Saint-Ouen flea market
(I go there often, searching for objects that can be found nowhere else:
old-fashioned, broken, useless, almost incomprehensible, even
perverse . . .)'

(ANDRÉ BRETON 'NADJA')

Jardin des Tuileries
The Saint-Ouen flea market

'The human heart, beautiful as a seismograph.'
(ANDRÉ BRETON 'NADJA')
Galien et Hippocrate, Antiquités Médicales, Boulevard Saint-Germain

'And love: how strangely comfortable love would find itself in this café
where everything contrives to provoke looks and glances.'
(LOUIS ARAGON 'PARIS PEASANT')
Café Les Deux Magots, Boulevard Saint-Germain

Quai aux Fleurs

Nor was his meeting with Jacqueline at the end of May 1934 entirely fortuitous. She had indeed written to him and was later surprised that the letter had remained undelivered, presumably by a waiter. She was perfectly aware who he was; her cousin, away doing his national service, had been in touch with Breton, had introduced her to his work and this had inspired her with the desire to meet him. He was not difficult to track down, either – 'Meanwhile, you can be sure of meeting me in Paris' – and, with his remarkable looks, easily recognizable. When eventually he follows her from the café and she turns to confront him, he may choose to see it as fortuitous, but in fact she has, for whatever essential reason, set it up.

Their long nocturnal walk through Paris, some twenty-four hours later, is beautifully described – a marvellous evocation of falling hopelessly in love, especially Breton's moment of indecision in Les Halles when he realizes it is not too late to turn back. Yet, despite Surrealist points of reference – the Tour Saint-Jacques in its scaffolding, for instance – the general feel is, in my view, more romantic than Surrealist. 'We have reached the Quai aux Fleurs just as the mass of rose-coloured earthenware pots arrive, on whose base all tomorrow's active seduction is predicted and concentrated.' Witty and perceptive, certainly, but Surreal? There are also observations that the younger Breton would have totally rejected; in Les Halles he deplores, albeit mildly, the invasion of the smart revellers in 'evening clothes, furs, and silks', contrasting them with 'the vigorous rhythms of honest work'. Is this the same Breton who, less than ten years before, has castigated toil with the utmost rigour and severely attacked poor Nadja for stating that the working people on the Métro during the rush-hour were 'good'? Of course, we all change, and the long if futile flirtation with the Communist Party had perhaps left its mark, but finally the Parisian night walk of section Four of *Mad Love* is, while certainly lyrical, almost conventional, despite the Surreal sauce that the author, rather methodically, ladles over it.

139

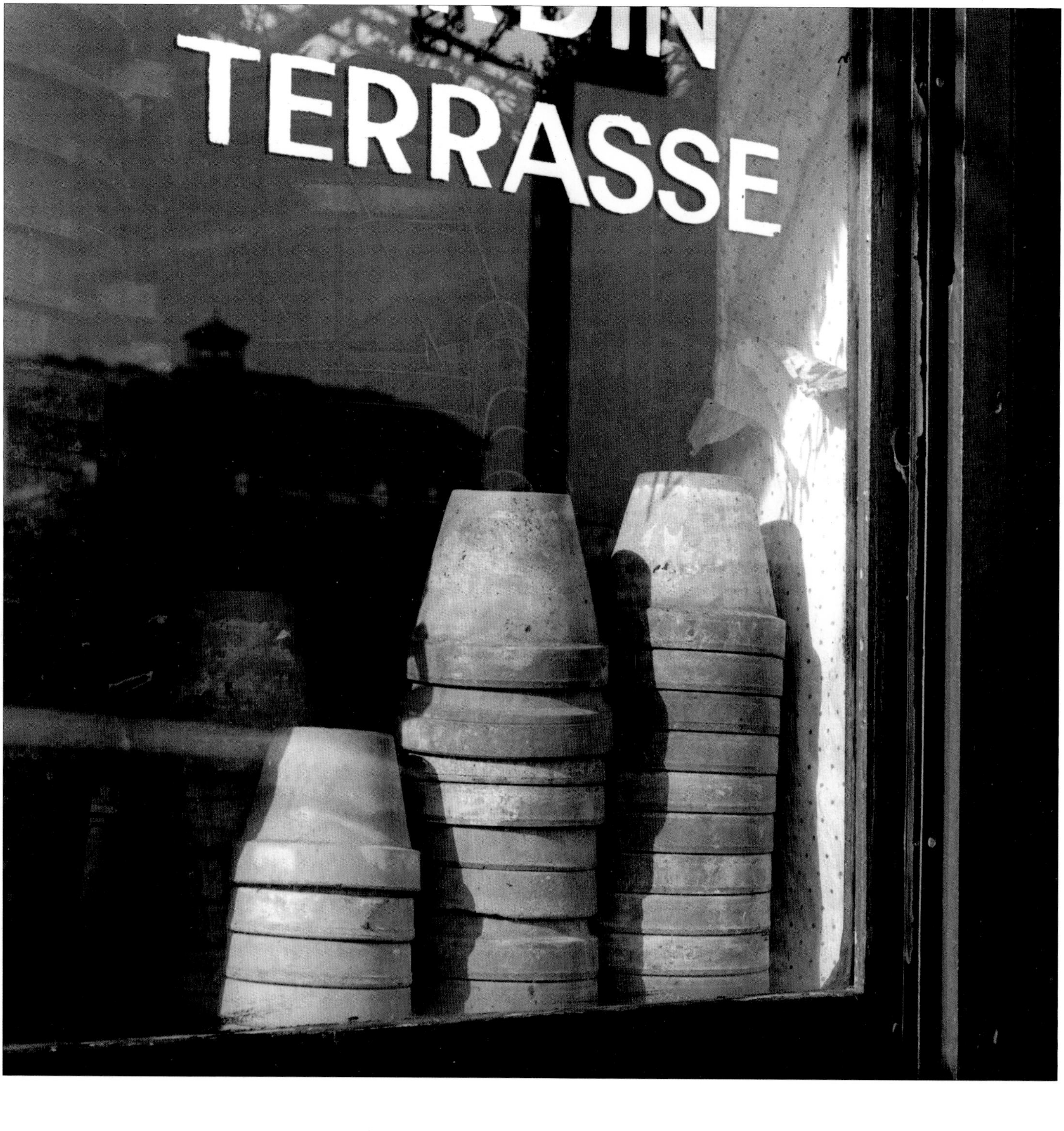
TERRASSE

'We have reached the Quai aux Fleurs just as the mass of rose-coloured earthenware pots arrive, on whose base all tomorrow's active seduction is predicted and concentrated.'

(ANDRÉ BRETON 'MAD LOVE')

Quai aux Fleurs

Les Halles, the Tour Saint-Jacques, the Hôtel de Ville, the Pont-au-Change, the Rue Gît-le-Coeur, the flower market, the Latin Quarter; it's a beautiful walk for lovers, but in retrospect Breton seems to realize that that, in itself, is not enough. It lacks another dimension. He finds it in an automatic poem he had written in 1923. It was called *Sunflower* (*Tournesol*) and indeed, without any forcing whatsoever, it would seem to presage, almost step-by-step, that walk of well over a decade later. There is even a reference to those who 'like that woman seem to be swimming'; and, as already stated, Jacqueline was a professional swimmer. It is, indeed, a remarkable piece of foresight in the full sense, guarding its secret until reality offered an exact parallel, and Breton's analysis is convincing in its clarity. Even so, I can't help being aware that it is something written in the heroic days of the Surrealist movement which transforms an elaborate piece of prose into something infinitely more mysterious. Loyalty, of course, forbids me even to contemplate that the route taken by Jacqueline Lamba and André Breton in 1934 might have been partially dictated by the unconscious memory of the places described in a poem of the early 'twenties, and anyway there is no explanation of the woman who swam in that poem and was to swim into the poet's life.

The section finishes with the words, 'The following August 14, I married the all-powerful commander of the night of the sunflower.' The rest of the book, much of it remarkable, and including a really disturbing ghost story, takes place far from Paris and need not concern us here.

Mad Love has many qualities, but I consider that in relation to Paris, it is closer to those lamentable pictures of Chagall where bendable couples and explosions of predictable bouquets float about in the vicinity of the Eiffel Tower, than to the soluble city of *Paris Peasant* and *Nadja*.

Quai aux Fleurs

'... Paris shown here in a quite specially organic and essential way
by its Hôtel de Ville, on our left as we walk towards the Latin
Quarter. I succumb to the wonderful dizziness these places inspire in
me, places where everything I have best known began.'

(ANDRÉ BRETON 'MAD LOVE')

Hôtel de Ville

'Let this curtain of shadows be lifted and let me be led fearlessly
towards the light!'

(ANDRÉ BRETON 'MAD LOVE')

Tour Saint-Jacques

5

'A majority of one'

*I*n 1952, and by now a professional jazz-singer, I returned to Paris for a few days with a telephone number and a letter of introduction from Mesens in my pocket. The first evening, with rather nervous awe, I rang up and made an appointment to visit André Breton at noon on the following day in the famous studio in the Rue Fontaine.

I was staying in Saint-Germain this time and decided to walk across Paris to Montmarte. It was a beautiful early autumn morning and I had several hours to fill. I carried with me the recently published *The Complete Nonsense of Edward Lear* and a bottle of white rum, Breton's favourite drink according to my briefing from E.L.T. On one of the quays I found, on a stall selling otherwise unremarkable old postcards, an Edwardian image of a nanny goat with a system of rubber tubes attached to its teats and a series of fat babies guzzling away at their extremities. I added it to my gifts.

Never had Paris seemed so beautiful to me, so tender and mysterious. I was in a state of exaltation, which several Pernods en route helped to reinforce; not exactly nervous, but out of myself. Ten years after opening Herbert Read's *Surrealism* in a Liverpool bookshop, and recognizing immediately that I had happened upon the key to a garden I had always suspected to exist, I was to meet the man who had forged that key. His voice on the telephone had been precise and neutral. Mesens, he said, had spoken of me. At last, on the first stroke of twelve, I checked with the concierge, who had been warned to expect me, crossed the courtyard, climbed the stairs and rang the bell.

Breton answered it and I followed him into a room which gave the impression of a musuem. Every object had its place, the walls were covered with pictures – Miró, Ernst, de Chirico – the

André Breton's house,
42 Rue Fontaine

Café Congrès, Place Blanche

furniture unremarkable. I remained there for three quarters of an hour and although my French is abominable and, as we know, Breton spoke no English, there seemed to be no difficulty in communicating; indeed, I almost had the illusion that the conversation was conducted in English. He thanked me gravely for the presents, inspecting the postcard of the babies suckled by a goat with solemn attention. He asked me about Surrealism in Britain. He apologized at being unable to show me a Dali – *The Old Age of William Tell* – because it was in the bedroom and his wife was still not dressed. As the picture contained a massive erection this, even at the time, struck me as odd.

Finally, when I claimed falsely that I had another appointment (I felt I might soon bore him), he suggested that I might be interested in attending a meeting that night in a café off the Place Blanche and, on my acceptance, took a piece of yellow writing-paper headed with the word *Medium*, the title of the Surrealist magazine then current, and wrote me directions as to how to get there in a clear, unaffected hand. It is one of my most bitter regrets that, after preserving it for many years, I am unable to find that scrap of paper, that talisman. We shook hands and I left.

Don't think I don't know that my description of this meeting has the hysterical absurdity of an enamoured schoolgirl confiding to her diary that she has met a pop star, but that is exactly how I felt. I've met many people I've admired in my life, but only Breton reduced me to such an absurd pitch of idolatry. I understood immediately why one erstwhile Surrealist wrote that 'leaving the movement was like breaking off a love affair'. I understand the bitterness of those expelled, the savagery of their attacks in exile. Breton emanated that much over-used word, charisma. His failings, particularly Aragon's witty definition of him 'always giving the impression of being in a majority of one', are obvious, but no one but he could have sustained an idealistic movement for so long. Even after his death, which in effect signalled its end, he left it on the wind to brush our temples and to remind us of at least the possibility of hope and freedom. That Breton was sometimes wrong and his opponents right is now irrelevant. He drew together or influenced many of the greatest creative imaginations of this century and under his severe gaze they produced their best work, were most truly themselves.

That evening I turned up at the time Breton had suggested to find him waiting for me. The group, due to a disagreement between Péret and a waiter (apparently a not uncommon occurrence), had decided to move to another café, and he had remained behind to show me the way. That I was impressed by his thoughtfulness is self-evident. At the large table I sat by the painter, Toyen, who spoke, as far as I can recall, excellent English, and I felt that my whole life had led up to this moment. Of course, I had attended many Surrealist meetings in London, but this was entirely different. I was in Paris and there sat André Breton as he had done ever since 1924, two years before I was born. It would, however, be hypocritical not to admit to feeling a little regretful that I hadn't taken my place some twenty years earlier when, instead of these noisy young men, all of them unknown to me and, naturally, uninterested in this Englishman unable to contribute to the polemics, I might have expected to see Éluard, Max Ernst, Miró, Tanguy and the still-acceptable Dali amongst many others, but nevertheless there I was.

I never met him again, although later on I got to know his wife Elisa and I frequently visit her. She is a most attractive and intelligent person, not without a certain abrasive wit very necessary in dealing with the burden of being a great man's widow. 'Last night', she told me once, 'a young man turned up in the courtyard bawling poetry in honour of André. It was two in the morning. Well really!' Naturally, she is plagued by researchers, thesis-writers, admirers, but she copes. She's not without her small acts of defiance too and often visits Greece. 'André', she explained, 'would never go there because it was the birthplace of reason, but I *love* it.' The studio, though, is kept like a shrine. Everything remains in exactly the same place. The desk is as it was that fine morning in the early 'fifties. Breton, if he were to enter the room, would find nothing changed. He could sit down, pick up his pen and again assume his task: the attempt to delineate 'the white curve on a black background that we call thought'.

The post-war years of Parisian Surrealism were not especially remarkable. Within the movement itself there were also desertions and expulsions for many reasons. Max Ernst, for example, was excommunicated for accepting the prize for painting at the Venice biennale, although his refusal to renounce his life-long friendship with Éluard was probably equally relevant.

'This is the month of Venus
This is the loveliest month of all.
The mind is trapped by these networks which lure him irretrievably
towards the final chapter in his destiny.'
(LOUIS ARAGON 'PARIS PEASANT')
The New Moon nightclub

There was a mass exodus when Breton tried to insist on the group's moral condemnation of Matta on the grounds that his affair with Gorky's wife had contributed to the suicide of that brilliant American artist; a curious notion indeed, given the central Surrealist belief that one should never be repudiated in *l'amour fou*.

Within a few years only the ever-faithful poet, Benjamin Péret, and the fine and underrated painter, Toyen, remained from the old guard. Those abroad – Mesens and Brunius in London, Magritte and his circle in Brussels – stayed loyal, as was comparatively easy at a distance, but in the main Breton presided over a gang of youngsters unlikely to question his authority, in particular one Schuster, whom Breton was to name his executor, and who was referred to by his enemies as 'the corporal'. As had always been the case, Breton's dominance or, as Aragon described it, the impression he gave of always being in the majority, contributed to the illusion of seamless uniformity that has constantly been stressed by enemies of the Surrealist movement. In an interview towards the end of his life, he added, 'André's *power* over me had become enhanced as the result of the constitution of a real Surrealist group that included newcomers who were younger than us and who were constantly trying to demonstrate their orthodoxy at the expense of Philippe [Soupault], Paul [Éluard] or myself.' In the early, heroic days when there had been some room for manoeuvre, as Aragon himself acknowledged, 'he was capable of reacting sharply against an automatic interpretation of his thoughts'. As time went on, of course, his papal omnipotence became more dominant. Either you agreed entirely with A.B., you left, or were pushed.

In contrast to the 'twenties and 'thirties, and the heroic if doomed attempt to reconcile the liberated imagination and effective political action, more and more stress was laid on arcane mysticism, alchemy (as a parallel to the transformation of words), and a belief in initiates – in direct contrast to Lautréamont's early assertion that 'poetry must be made by all'. There were still protests, most of them valid, against French colonialism, Stalinist tyranny, De Gaulle, consumerism. There were large exhibitions, but no great new talents emerged, and the paintings and sculpture of the past, the found and interpreted objects, were already entering museums or beginning to acquire substantial value; a millstone around the neck of a movement still aiming to operate effectively in the present. The 'scandalous' weapon had rusted beyond use; Breton complained wryly that it was impossible to shock anybody any more. Former Surrealists had begun to publish 'histories'. A photograph of Breton and his young turks protesting at the installation of Picasso's (very bad) bust in memory of Apollinaire in the precincts of l'Église Saint-Germain appears touching, but also rather quaint. Breton himself admitted that if a new movement were to arise that seemed to him relevant and potentially effective he would offer his support.

No such movement was forthcoming, and in 1966, taken ill in his medieval house in Saint Cirq-Lapopie, near Cahors, he was rushed to Paris and, on 28 September, he died.

Breton's cortège was followed by a great crowd of young people, to the astonishment of those, both friend and foe alike, who had imagined him forgotten, but there was to be a more extraordinary homage in 1968. When the students took to the streets and, to the consternation of the Gaullists and Communists alike, made their 'impossible' demands, their slogans were drawn not from Marx, Lenin or even Sartre, but from Breton and the Surrealists.

6

'A calla lily'

On that same trip to Paris that I described in Chapter One, I decided to lay a calla lily on Breton's grave: 'In the sky despair was swirling its great calla lilies so lovely' (*Sunflower*). I knew already that, unlike many of his companions, he wasn't buried in the Père-Lachaise, that huge city of the dead with its hundred thousand cadavers and the ashes of a million more, but in a comparatively small cemetery to the north of Montmartre, and this at his own request so that he could lie close to the faithful Péret. Michael Woods had already photographed the stone and described it to me, but I had foolishly mislaid the name of the location.

I asked at the little cemetery in Montmartre itself, first buying my calla lily in a smart flower shop at its gates, and an official, who knew exactly who Breton was, said that he believed he was buried at the Cimetière de Saint-Ouen. When we got there in a taxi soon after midday, there was nobody to ask but an elderly and abrupt caretaker wearing a shabby uniform and very small metal spectacles. He had also clearly suffered at some point from a severe stroke, which made him very difficult to understand. He had never heard of Breton. What he did tell us – that the office was closed for lunch but would be open again at two – was interrupted by the emergence from amongst the tombs of a plump, badly dressed man with blood streaming down his face, but otherwise perfectly cheerful, who was eventually led off by our non-informant in search of medication.

So we went and had lunch in an excellent workman's café close to the flea market, which had played so important a role in Breton's life, and then returned, via a street lined with florists and shops selling kitsch monumental masonry, to the ornate gates of the burying ground and the now-open office beyond.

Parc Monceau

Only there was no André Breton buried there – although, strangely enough, their files yielded an André Le Breton who had died in 1912. Even so, on their professional mettle and sensing perhaps our disappointment, symbolized by the now fast-wilting calla lily, they began to ring up other cemeteries and at last established that it was the Cimetière des Batignolles we were looking for. Furthermore, a young employee in a black leather jacket offered us a lift there in his car. It was, he told us, not far away.

When we arrived, via a motorway encircling the city, he dived into the office and returned with a map and, on the back, a list of those considered important enough to be singled out. Compared to the Père-Lachaise, which houses everyone from Balzac to Jim Morrison, it was undersubscribed. Here it is:

DIRECTION DES PARCS,
JARDINS ET ESPACES VERTS

SECTION DES CIMETIERES

4, rue d'Aubervilliers - 75019 PARIS

Tél. : 42-00-33-15

Ville de Paris
—
Cimetière des Batignolles

8 rue Saint-Just (17ª)

Index des CELEBRITES

① ALENÇON (Emilienne d´) Marthe André   1ª Division
② BRETON André : Poète   31ª Division
③ BREVAL Lucienne : Actrice—   2ª Division
④ GRASSET : Amiral   28ª Division
⑤ PELADAN Joseph : Ecrivain _ Mage   6ª Division
⑥ SAINT-GRANIER : Chansonnier   13ª Division
⑦ VERLAINE Paul : Poète   20ª Division
⑧ VORELLI : Chanteur   30ª Division

Verlaine, at any rate because of his connection with Rimbaud, was in keeping, but the rest suggest a happy incongruity which might have pleased Breton more. It is sad, though, that the authorities have not yet seen fit to include Péret, a fine poet and faithful unto death, amongst these comparatively modest

'CELEBRITES'. Indeed, although we searched for Péret's grave we couldn't find it, but Michael assures me it's there.

Our friend deposited us at the foot of Breton's last resting place and zoomed off to his place of work. It's a simple, rather gritty slab with, in one corner, a clumsy carving of a geometrical, star-like shape. Above it, a short distance away, the *autoroute* traffic roared overhead. I laid down my by-now battered lily.

On the stone is carved:

André Breton
1896 – 1966
'Je cherche l'or du temps'

Next morning we left the Hôtel des Grands Hommes in plenty of time to catch the plane, only to find there was both a Métro and taxi strike. At the last minute, however, a blackleg cab stopped and agreed, at a considerable price, to try and get us there.

En route, I happened to glance out of the window. We were travelling very fast along a motorway and below us, at that precise moment, was the Cimetière des Batignolles where Breton lies under that moving inscription. And beyond that lies Montmartre and the whole city of Paris where he and his companions not only sought for gold, but mined it for the enrichment of us all.

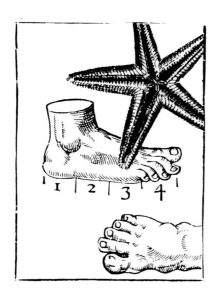

Bibliography

Books consulted or quoted by the author
(the dates are of the edition used)

Sarane Alexandrian, *Surrealist Art*, Thames
and Hudson, London and New York
1978

Ferdinand Alquié, *The Philosophy of
Surrealism*, translated by Bernard
Waldrop, University of Michigan Press,
Ann Arbor 1965

Louis Aragon, *Paris Peasant*, translated by
Simon Watson Taylor, Picador, London
1987

André Breton, *Mad Love*, translated by Mary
Ann Caws, University of Nebraska Press,
Lincoln and London 1987

— — *Nadja*, translated by Richard Howard,
Grove Press, New York 1960

— — *Poems of André Breton: a bilingual
anthology*, translated and edited by Jean-
Pierre Cauvin and Mary Ann Caws,
University of Texas Press, Austin 1982

Roger Cardinal, 'The Soluble City – the
Surrealist perception of Paris',
Architectural Design 48, nos 2–3 (1978)

— — *Breton, Nadja*, Grant and Cutler,
London 1986

Roger Cardinal and Robert Short,
Surrealism: permanent revelation, Studio
Vista, London 1970

Wallace Fowlie, *Age of Surrealism*, Indiana
University Press, Bloomington 1960

Johann Friedrich Geist, *Arcades: the history
of a building type*, MIT Press, London 1985

Malcolm Haslam, *The real world of the
Surrealists*, Weidenfeld & Nicolson,
London 1978

Marcel Jean (editor), *The Autobiography of
Surrealism*, Viking, London 1980

J.H. Matthews, *Languages of Surrealism*,
University of Missouri Press, Columbia
1986

Gaetan Picon, *Surrealists and Surrealism,
1919–1939*, Skira, Geneva 1977

Hans Richter, *Dada: Art and Anti-Art*,
Thames and Hudson, London and New
York 1965

NADJA by André Breton, translated by
Richard Howard. Copyright © 1960,
1988 by Grove Press, Inc. Used by
permission of Grove Weidenfeld, a
division of Grove Press, Inc., John
Calder (Publishers) Ltd, London.

PARIS PEASANT by Louis Aragon,
translated by Simon Watson Taylor.
Copyright © 1987 by Jonathan Cape
Ltd. Used by permission of Jonathan
Cape Ltd and Editions Gallimard, Paris.

Index

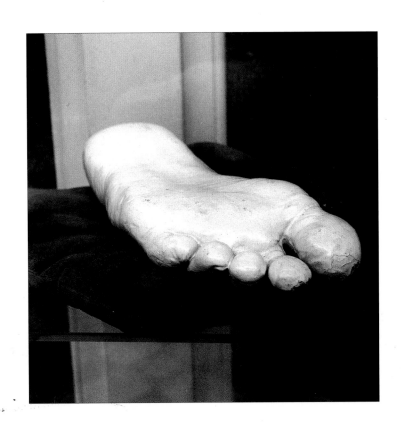

COURBEVOIE

CLICHY

LEVALLOIS-PERRET

NEUILLY

Pont de Neuilly

Jardin d'Acclimatation

BOULOGNE

Boulevard Maillot

Avenue de Neuilly

Boulevard Eugène

Chemin de Fer de l'Ouest

Pte de Clichy

Av. de Clichy

Boul. Bessières

Stn. de l'Av. de Clichy

Stn. du St.

Cimetière Montmartre

Pte d'Asnières

Pte de Courcelles

Boulevard Berthier

Stn. des Batignolles

Ste Marie des Batignolles

Place de Clichy

Rue de Clichy

Pte de Champerret

Pte de Villiers

Pte des Ternes

Chap. St Ferd.

Pte Maillot

Station de la Pte Maillot

Stn. de Courcelles

Av. Niel

Av. de Wagram

Av. de Villiers

Boul. de Courcelles

Parc de Monceaux

Théâtre

Col. Chaptal

B. des Batignolles

St Augustin

Gare St Lazare

Boulevard Haussmann

Hôpital Beaujon

Av. Friedland

Arc de Triomphe

Étoile

Avenue des Champs-Élysées

Palais de l'Élysée

Faubg St Honoré

Madeleine

B. d. Cap.

Ste H. St Roch

Pl. Vendôme

Av. du Bois de Boulogne

Av. d'Eylau

Avenue Kléber

Avenue Marceau

Av. de l'Alma

Av. Montaigne

Palais de l'Industrie

Pl. de la Concorde

Jardin des Tuileries

Pte Dauphine

Station de la Pte Dauphine

Avenue Malakoff

Cours la Reine

Pt des Reine

Av. de la Grande Armée

R. des Dames

Pte de la Muette

Station

La Muette

R. de Passy

Station de Passy

Pl. du Trocadéro

Quai de Passy

Pont d'Iéna

Quai d'Orsay

Mané des Tabacs

Espl. des Inval.

Chambe d. Députés

Pte de l'Alma

Invalides

St Clotilde

Boulevard des Invalides

Pte de Passy

Av. Ingres

Boulevard Suchet

Chemin de Fer

Ceinture

Station de Passy

R. de Passy

Rue Raynouard

Rue La Fontaine

Champ de Mars

École Militaire

Av. de la Bourdonnaye

Av. de Suffren

Hôtel des Invalides

Pl. Vauban

Av. de Breteuil

Av. de Tourville

Hôpital Temporaire

Gare d'Auteuil

R. d'Auteuil

Quai de Versailles

Quai de Grenelle

Boulevard de Grenelle

Boulevard de Vaugirard

Rue Saint Charles

Rue de Lourmel

Rue Croix Nivert

St Jean Bapte de Gren.

Boul. de Grenelle

St Lambert

Gare Montparnasse (de l'Ouest)

N. D. des

Cimetière du Mont-Parnasse

Boul. Excelmans

B. Murat

Station du Point du Jour

Pte de Sèvres

Stn. de Grenelle

Av. Murat

Boul. Victor